"The sights, sounds, smells, symbols, and rituals of the liturgical seasons are powerful "tools" for helping children grow in faith. In *Celebrating Seasons: Prayer Lessons for Advent, Christmas, Lent, and Easter* the authors make the most of all these tools through creative activities and meaningful prayer services that involve the whole child. Each of these celebrations offers an experience of the season that will remain in the participants' minds and hearts. Excellent material for religion classes, for family celebrations, and for intergenerational parish celebrations."

Alison Berger
Editor, *Religion Teacher's Journal*

"Calendars can and often do dictate rather than direct. When they dictate we lose sight of meaning and spontaneity as we immerse ourselves in the rigors we call life's treadmill. God speaks and God creates in the ordinary moments and movements of life, in the cycles of life's (and the church's) seasons. From readings to pizza parties, rituals to reflections, the authors give us new glimpses and new opportunities for the festival half of the church's calendar. Opportunities, yes, but more than that. They are occasions to taste God's presence in our lives. This is a book for children (including children over 21!). It holds a wealth of treasures for individual families, classes, and worship settings."

The Rev. Dr. Richard B. Gilbert, BBC
Executive Director, The World Pastoral Care Center
and Director of Chaplaincy Services, Sherman Hospital
Elgin, Illinois

"I love this book! Very helpful! Very needed."

J. Kok
Crystal Cathedral

CELEBRATING SEASONS

SEASONS

Prayer Lessons for Advent Christmas Lent and Easter

Phyllis Vos Wezeman
Jude Dennis Fournier

TWENTY-THIRD PUBLICATIONS
BAYARD Mystic, CT 06355

Twenty-Third Publications/ Bayard
185 Willow Street
P.O. Box 180
Mystic, CT 06355
(860) 536-2611
(800) 321-0411

ISBN:1-58595-016-5
Library of Congress Catalog Card Number: 99-48984
Printed in the U.S.A.

Contents

Introduction

What would life be like without calendars? These useful organizational tools help provide the structure for many aspects of our lives. Just as the secular calendar reminds us that it's time for Valentine hearts or Thanksgiving turkeys, the church calendar invites us to observe the great festivals of faith such as Advent, Christmas, Epiphany, Lent, Easter, and Pentecost.

From Advent through Pentecost, we experience in a special way the life and ministry of Jesus as he empowered his church to carry on the work God began in creation. The Scripture stories which recount the life of Jesus become part of the rhythm of our lives, anticipated, celebrated, savored, and shared by all God's people. Rather than treasured fragments of disconnected text, the Bible is the woven fabric of a seamless garment, the underpinnings of our liturgical year. And so each season of the church year flows meaningfully to the next, completing the cycle even as it leads us to begin again the wonderful journey of faithful discipleship.

Celebrating Seasons: Prayer Lessons for Advent, Christmas, Lent, and Easter will help children experience and explore various aspects of and approaches to prayer as they relate to themes of the church year. For each season, a new focus is developed to help students experience, understand, and appreciate the events of that season in creative, concrete, and challenging ways.

Each lesson is designed in an easy-to-use format, and organized into three parts. "Goal" states the purpose of the activity, "Gather" lists the materials required and suggests steps for advance preparation, and "Guide" contains complete directions for sharing the experience. Methods that involve the students in the learning process are emphasized.

These lessons are ideal for religious education classes, Catholic school programs, children's liturgy of the Word, vacation Bible school, retreats, and intergenerational events. While these lessons are intended for young people in classroom settings, they may be easily adapted for use in small and large group prayer or other religious education, outreach, and nurture opportunities. They can also be used by families within the home.

May all who use this resource rediscover the message and the meaning of the seasons of the church year in interesting, inviting, and involving ways.

Overview of the Church Year

Advent

Advent falls during the four weeks prior to Christmas. During Advent, the church prepares to celebrate the historical birth of Jesus as a babe in a manger, and for the rebirth of Christ's presence in the hearts of faithful people. Advent is also a time to remember that we wait for Christ's promised return to the world, called the parousia, or "second coming."

The lectionary readings for Advent focus on prophecy, especially Isaiah's foretelling of the Messiah and John the Baptist's announcements of the need for repentance and preparation for the One who is to come. The color for Advent is usually purple or dark blue, representing both the darkness of the world without Christ and the royal colors fit for a king.

Christmas

The Christmas season begins on December twenty-fifth, and is celebrated through the feast of the Baptism of the Lord. During this time, carols are sung, the Christmas story read, and the birth of Jesus celebrated. The color for the Christmas season is usually white.

There are other important feasts within the Christmas season. The first of these is the feast of the Holy Family. This occurs on the first Sunday after Christmas, and emphasizes the goodness of Joseph, Mary, and Jesus. The feast of the Holy Family encourages all Christian families to follow the model of the Holy Family by their attention to prayer, good works, and most important of all, the love and care of all members of our families.

January 1 is the Solemnity of the Blessed Virgin Mary, Mother of God, while the feast of the Epiphany is celebrated on January 6. In many dioceses today, however, the Epiphany is celebrated on the second Sunday after Christmas.

Epiphany literally means "appearance" or "revelation." On this day, Christians celebrate the arrival of the wise men from the East in Bethlehem. This event signifies God's gift—Jesus—being made available to all people throughout the world. It is a time to celebrate new revelations of God's presence among us.

The appropriate color for the feast of the Epiphany is white, although gold is sometimes used to represent the color of the star and the gift brought to the Christ child.

The Sunday following the Epiphany is known as the Baptism of the Lord, and it marks the end of the Christmas season. (When the Epiphany is celebrated on the second Sunday after Christmas, and that Sunday falls on January 7 or 8, the Baptism of the Lord is observed on the next day, Monday.)

Lent

Like Advent, Lent is a season of preparation. Historically, this was the time set aside for new converts to prepare for baptism. It was also a time for Christians who had committed serious sins to do penance and be restored. During Lent, fasting, prayer, and self-examination were encouraged as spiritual disciplines—as they are to this day. Sundays, however, were treated as feastdays when the fast and penance could be suspended.

Lectionary readings during Lent include the recounting of the forty days Jesus wandered in the desert after his baptism; the Transfiguration story; and stories of Jesus' encounters with religious leaders that relate to Jesus' own awareness of his mission and its consequences. The challenge to spend forty days in reflection and spiritual discipline parallels the message of the season.

Ash Wednesday marks the beginning of this time of preparation. Palms from the previous year are burned and mixed with oil to make the ashes placed on our foreheads as a sign of humility.

The Sunday before Easter is known as Palm Sunday and commemorates Jesus' triumphant entry into Jerusalem, as well as the beginning of Holy Week. Holy Thursday celebrates the institution of the Eucharist, which stems from the Passover seder Jesus shared with his disciples. Good Friday marks the paradoxical nature of Jesus' death: while the suffering of the crucifixion can hardly be called "good," the atonement for sin and the gift of salvation through Christ's sacrifice is good news for all Christians. Lent ends with the celebration of the Easter Vigil on Holy Saturday.

The color for Lent is purple, a color that reminds us of the darkness of our sin as well as the royalty of Jesus. The color for both Palm Sunday and Good Friday is red; for Holy Thursday, it is white.

Easter

The season of Easter begins with the Easter Vigil liturgy, usually held after darkness falls on Holy Saturday. During this liturgy, symbols of light and darkness dramatically convey the passage of Jesus from death to resurrection. At the Vigil, the sacraments of baptism, confirmation, and first Eucharist are often conferred on those who have been preparing for them through the RCIA. Lectionary readings for this liturgy emphasize the origins of the Christian faith rooted in Judaism and the Hebrew people.

The actual date for Easter changes each year based on the cycles of the moon. Easter Sunday is the first Sunday after the first full moon after the vernal equinox which occurs around March 21. Thus, Easter can be as early as March 22 and as late as April 25.

The first Easter was established based on the Jewish celebration of the Passover. The Orthodox churches continue to use Passover as the determining date for Easter services; their Palm Sunday occurs the first Sunday after Passover begins. Additionally, some scholars say the day for Easter was set to assure that the light of the moon would be available to pilgrims who traveled to Jerusalem at this time.

Easter is not just one Sunday, however; it is a season which lasts for fifty days.

During the season of Easter, the resurrection is celebrated and stories of Jesus' appearances to the disciples are told. The promise of the gift of the Spirit and the challenge to "go out into all the world" are a part of the Easter season. The feast of the Ascension falls forty days after Easter Sunday.

The color for the Easter season is white.

Pentecost

At the Jewish harvest festival of Pentecost, fifty days after Easter, God sent the gift of the Holy Spirit to the community of believers left on earth. The Spirit's coming was marked by a mighty wind that moved the disciples from the upper room out into the marketplace.

The Spirit was also seen as tongues of fire that danced above the disciples and infused them with the power to share the story of Jesus in whatever language the listening crowd could understand. A third symbol of Pentecost became a descending dove representing baptism and the quiet presence of the Spirit.

Pentecost is considered the birthday of the church, when Peter preached the first sermon and the first converts were made. This feast focuses on the importance of the Christian mission. Lectionary readings include Jesus' teachings to the disciples, especially his challenge to go forth in mission and to share God's love. "What does it mean to be a Christian?" and "What does it mean to be the church?" are questions appropriate for the feast of Pentecost.

The color for Pentecost is red, symbolizing the fire of enthusiasm and the force of energy that comes with empowerment by God.

The Sunday after Pentecost is called Trinity Sunday, in recognition that God's revelation is now complete as God the Creator, or Father; God the Redeemer, or Son; and God the Sanctifier, or Holy Spirit. On the following Sunday, we mark the feast of the Body and Blood of Christ.

Ordinary Time

Ordinary time begins on the Sunday after the Baptism of the Lord, and continues to Ash Wednesday. It then resumes on the Sunday following the feast of the Body and Blood of Christ, and ends with the feast of Christ the King, which falls on the Sunday before Advent begins.

Ordinary time is a season of discipleship and growth. Lectionary readings focus on following in Christ's footsteps and becoming who God would have us be. Involvement in the church and Christian responsibility are two of the challenges to consider during Ordinary time. Our own personal growth and spiritual nurture should lead to outreach and ministry as we become disciples who offer the good news of Jesus and the hand of service.

The color for Ordinary time is green.

Counting the Days

Goal

To create an Advent calendar and to use it to review Old Testament prophecies and New Testament fulfillments related to the birth of Jesus.

Gather

- Construction paper
- Scissors
- Bible(s)
- Fine-tipped markers
- Pencils and pens

- Glue or tape
- Patterns for Advent calendar
- "Prophecies and Fulfillments" list
- Paper
- Duplicating equipment

Advance Preparation

- Prepare copies of the Advent calendar patterns.
- Reproduce the "Prophecies and Fulfillments" list

Guide

The promise of a Savior is recorded in Scripture from as early as Genesis, the first book of the Bible. Throughout the entire Old Testament, numerous predictions of the Promised One are given.

As a way to review Old Testament prophecies and their fulfillment in the New Testament, create Advent calendars that will also help the children count the days to Christmas. Hand out the "Prophecies and Fulfillments" list and discuss several of the Scripture passages with the students. Next, guide the process

of preparing the two pieces of the calendar. Distribute the calendar patterns. Note that the top sheet contains the numbered windows to open each day and the bottom piece shows the Scripture passages.

Invite the students to choose a piece of construction paper to use for the base of the calendar. Refer to the "Prophecies and Fulfillments" list and direct them to print one Scripture reference in each square. Be sure the words are positioned in the order in which they are to be read (one through twenty-five).

When the bottom piece of the calendar is completed, tell the students to select another sheet of construction paper to use as the top portion of the card. Instruct the group to prepare the top sheet by drawing the windows and numbering them from one to twenty-five. Guide the process of carefully cutting each window on three sides. Show the group how to position the sheet with the windows over the paper with the words. Place glue in each corner to stick the two pieces together, or run tape along the outside edges of the calendar.

Review the process for using the calendars. On the first day of Advent, open window number one. Locate the Scripture passage in a Bible and read the verse(s). Note that for the first twenty days a prophecy will be read one day, followed by its fulfillment the next. The last five passages record the events surrounding the birth of Jesus.

Tell the group to continue opening one window each day, revealing window twenty-five on Christmas Day. As each window is opened, suggest that the students recite a prayer such as, "Thank you, God, for keeping your promises" or "Thank you for sending Jesus, our Savior."

Prophecies & Fulfillments from Scripture

Offspring of a woman
Prophecy: Genesis 3:15
Fulfillment: Galatians 4:4

Promised offspring of Abraham
Prophecy: Genesis 18:18
Fulfillment: Acts 3:25

Promised offspring of Isaac
Prophecy: Genesis 17:19
Fulfillment: Matthew 1:2

Promised offspring of Jacob
Prophecy: Numbers 24:17
Fulfillment: Luke 3:34

Descend from the tribe of Judah
Prophecy: Genesis 49:10
Fulfillment: Luke 3:33

Heir to the throne of David
Prophecy: Isaiah 9:7
Fulfillment: Matthew 1:1

Place of birth
Prophecy: Micah 5:2
Fulfillment: Matthew 2:1

Time of birth
Prophecy: Daniel 9:25
Fulfillment: Luke 2:1–2

Born of a virgin
Prophecy: Isaiah 7:14
Fulfillment: Matthew 1:18

Slaughter of the infants
Prophecy: Jeremiah 31:15
Fulfillment: Matthew 2:16

Annunciation to Mary
Luke 1:26–38

The angel appears to Joseph
Matthew 1:18–25

Mary visits Elizabeth
Luke 1:39–56

Birth of Jesus
Luke 2:1–7

Visit of the shepherds
Luke 2:8–17

Top piece of calendar

			4	5
6	7	8	9	10
11	12	13	14	15

bottom piece of calendar

Waiting for Jesus

Goal

To understand that waiting helps people get ready for something that is coming, just as the season of Advent helps people prepare to celebrate the birth of Jesus.

Gather

- Table
- Candle (white)
- Matches
- Newsprint
- 3" x 5" index cards
- Bible(s)
- Cassette or CD of Christmas music (without words)

- Prayer cloth (blue or purple)
- Blue or purple ribbon
- Wicker basket
- Markers
- Pencils or pens
- Cassette or CD player

Advance Preparation

• Set the table in a prominent place in the room. Arrange the tablecloth, candle, and wicker basket on the table.

Guide

Advent, the four-week season prior to Christmas, is a time of waiting for the coming of Christ. During Advent, the church waits to remember the birth of Jesus as a babe in a manger, and for the rebirth of Christ's presence in the hearts of faithful people. Advent is also a time to remember that we wait for Christ's promised return to the world, called the parousia, or "second coming."

Explain to the students that waiting is an important part of life. "Waiting" may be defined as: "to remain until something expected happens; to be ready." Waiting offers people the opportunity to prepare for something that is expected to happen.

Invite the group to brainstorm a list of things or events for which people wait. Use chalk or markers to record the ideas on a chalkboard or on a large piece of newsprint. Encourage the students to develop a list of twenty-five items, one for each day leading up to and including Christmas.

Once the list has been completed, invite the children to discuss the theme of waiting. Ask when waiting is easy and when waiting is hard. Remind the group that waiting allows people an opportunity to get ready, or to prepare, for that which is coming. The season of Advent is a special time to prepare for the birth of Jesus.

Ask the students to gather around the prayer table. As the group sits in silence, play reflective Advent or Christmas instrumental music and light the candle. Invite the group to think of one way they will use the season of Advent as a time to "wait" for the birth of Jesus at Christmas. For example: I will pray everyday; I will take care of my sister so my mother and father can write Christmas cards; I will send a letter to my grandfather; I will not "bug" my parents to buy a certain toy.

Distribute index cards and pencils or pens and direct the students to write their statement on the card. Continue to play music during this time. When everyone has completed a card, lead the group in a brief prayer experience (see next page for a suggested setting).

Suggestions might be:
- Allowance
- Birthdays
- Christmas
- Fresh baked cookies
- Friends
- Line at amusement park
- Mail
- Movies
- New baby brother or sister
- Parties
- Performances
- Phone calls
- Pizza delivery
- Recess
- School bus
- Snow
- Store clerks/lines
- Sunrise/sunset
- Toast to pop
- Traffic lights
- Transportation (airplanes/boats/cars/trains)
- Turns (games/talking)
- Vacation
- Visit from/to Grandma or Grandpa
- Water to boil

Advent Prayer Service

Opening Prayer

God, friend to all who long to see your face, we gather in anticipation of Christmas and the glorious coming of your son, Jesus. We wait in patience for that day of great joy so we may experience the fullness of your love. We pray this in the name of Jesus, the Messiah. Amen.

Scripture Reading   *James 5:7–10*

Be patient, therefore, beloved, until the coming of the Lord. The farmer waits for the precious crop from the earth, being patient with it until it receives the early and the late rains. You also must be patient. Strengthen your hearts, for the coming of the Lord is near. Beloved, do not grumble against one another, so that you may not be judged. See, the Judge is standing at the doors! As an example of suffering and patience, beloved, take the prophets who spoke in the name of the Lord.

Prayer Response   *Based on Psalm 80*

ALL   Lord, we wait in longing, let us see your face.

Reader   O shepherd of Israel, hearken from your throne, shine forth. Rouse your power, and come to us who wait.

ALL   Lord, we wait in longing, let us see your face.

Reader   Once again, O Lord, look down from heaven, and see;
Take care of this vine, and protect what your right hand has planted.

ALL   Lord, we wait in longing, let us see your face.

Action Response

Invite the participants to approach the table, one at a time, and to place their prayer card in the basket.

Closing Prayer

Conclude by standing around the prayer table, joining hands, and reciting the Lord's Prayer.

Employing Our Senses

Goal

To allow our faith to "come to our senses" during the seasons of Advent, Christmas, and Epiphany.

Gather

- Paper
- Duplicating equipment
- Bible(s)

Guide

We often emphasize the mission Jesus calls us to by saying, "Go out into all the world." Even so, we must remember that Jesus' first word to the disciples was "Come." Nurture is perhaps the first and most important commitment of the church to its flock: shepherding, training, educating—in a word, "discipling."

The seasons of Advent and Christmas, which mark the beginning of the Christian story, are a good time to gather in and nurture people of all ages, especially children.

This prayer lesson will help students explore ways to allow faith to "come to our senses." Some children are inspired by seeing, others by hearing, and still others by touching, tasting, or smelling. A theme that focuses on all of the senses provides a variety of experiential learning opportunities, thus involving the students through the sense most suitable to each person's individual style.

In the following activities, all five senses are employed to help participants remember the story, comprehend its meaning, and express the joy of the gospel message.

Try these suggestions as the basis for a classroom prayer service or at a children's liturgy of the Word. They may also be sent home as a family project, or further developed into a program that spans the Advent and Christmas seasons.

Listen
Sense: Sound

Incline your ear, and come to me; listen, so that you may live. (Isaiah 55:3a)

Advent
Listen for God during Advent by learning a new way to pray. Instead of closing and folding hands in prayer, hold palms up and open during quiet time.

Christmas
Listen for the gift of loving words during the Christmas season. Instead of brushing compliments or praise aside, receive the words with humility as gifts from God.

Epiphany
Listen for new ideas with an open mind. Tune in a Christian radio or television program to hear how God's love is being revealed in the world.

Breathe
Sense: Smell

The spirit of God has made me, and the breath of the Almighty gives me life.
(Job 33:4)

Advent
Continue to learn new attitudes for prayer: while sitting quietly with palms open, breathe in the presence of God and exhale concerns and worries.

Christmas
While hurrying through the celebrations of Christmas, pause to record memories of Christmas in the air: breathe in and savor the seasonal smells outside, in the kitchen, and around the tree.

Epiphany
Fill the season with fragrant offerings like the magi's gift of frankincense. Burn candles, light incense, display potpourri to create fragrant memories of God's presence.

Savor
Sense: Taste

O taste and see that the Lord is good; happy are those who take refuge in him.
(Psalm 34:8)

Advent
During Advent, take the time to share a favorite dish or baked good with someone else. Enjoy the pleasure that comes from sharing.

Christmas
Invite someone who otherwise might be alone to share the tastes of your Christmas table.

Epiphany
Experiment with recipes for dishes from other cultures and celebrate Christ's birth for all the world.

Feel

Sense: Touch

She said to herself, "If I only touch his cloak, I will be made well."

> *(Matthew 9:21)*

Advent
Offer to massage the shoulders of someone weary with the Christmas rush—and if they want to return the favor and massage your shoulders, smile and say "Thanks!"

Christmas
Hold hands with loved ones as you share Christmas memories.

Epiphany
Exchange handmade gifts from third world countries and bless the hands who crafted each item.

Look

Sense: Sight

My eyes have seen your salvation.

> *(Luke 2:30)*

Advent
Prepare to see the meaning of Christmas more clearly this year by doing some spiritual reading each day of Advent.

Christmas
Visit churches to view their manger scenes and to appreciate the lights and displays of the season.

Epiphany
Go out each evening to view the stars, remembering the star that guided the magi to find Jesus. Ask God to guide your seeking.

Holding the Light

Goal

To use a guided meditation based on the story of Joseph, Mary, baby Jesus, and the shepherds to light the Advent and Christmas candles.

Gather

- Bible(s)
- Tablecloth (blue or purple)
- One white candle (in a holder)
- Basket of straw
- Cassette or CD player
- Cassette or CD of instrumental Advent or Christmas music
- Christmas card or picture depicting Joseph, Mary, baby Jesus, and the shepherds
- Table
- Advent wreath
- Matches
- Wooden manger

Advance Preparation

- Place the table in a prominent place in the room; cover with a blue or purple cloth.
- Arrange the Advent wreath, picture, basket of straw, and wooden manger on the table. Place the white candle in the middle of the Advent wreath.

Guide

Advent wreaths come in a variety of styles. One common arrangement is a circle of evergreen branches with three purple or dark blue candles and one pink candle placed around the circle. Sometimes, a white candle is placed in the center, to be lit on Christmas Eve or Christmas Day.

Invite the children to share in the preparation for Christmas by using an Advent wreath at school or home. Use this prayer service, based on the story of Joseph, Mary, baby Jesus, and the shepherds, on or near Christmas Eve as the culmination of the Advent season. To begin, ask the students to quietly gather around the prayer table.

Opening Song

O Come, O Come Emmanuel

Opening Prayer

Look to the Light
Condra Cadle

No deep darkness in the world
Can overcome the light:
A single candle flame will burn
Against the darkest night.

Let all the world of darkness come,
Resentment, envy, fears,
Then light the single flame of love;
The darkness disappears!

Scripture Reading: *Luke 2:4–16*

Light the first candle on the Advent wreath.

> Joseph also went from the town of Nazareth in Galilee to Judea, to the city of David called Bethlehem, because he was descended from the house and family of David. He went to be registered with Mary, to whom he was engaged and who was expecting a child.

Light the second Advent candle.

> While they were there, the time came for her to deliver her child. And she gave birth to her firstborn son and wrapped him in bands of cloth, and laid him in a manger, because there was no place for them in the inn.

Light the third Advent candle.

> In that region there were shepherds living in the fields, keeping watch over their flock by night. Then an angel of the Lord stood before them, and the glory of the Lord shone around them, and they were terrified. But the angel said to them, "Do not be afraid; for see—I am bringing you good news of great joy for all the people: to you is born this day in the city of David a Savior, who is the Messiah, the Lord. This will be a sign for you: you will find a child wrapped in bands of cloth and lying in a manger." And suddenly there was with the angel a multitude of the heavenly host, praising God and saying, "Glory to God in the highest heaven, and on earth peace among those whom he favors!"

Light the fourth Advent candle.

When the angels had left them and gone into heaven, the shepherds said to one another, "Let us go now to Bethlehem and see this thing that has taken place, which the Lord has made known to us." So they went with haste and found Mary and Joseph, and the child lying in the manger.

Guided Meditation

Invite the students to sit comfortably, to close their eyes, and to take part in a guided meditation. Read slowly, pausing briefly after each sentence. If desired, play tranquil Advent or Christmas instrumental music during the reading.

At this holy time of the year, come and let us join in a special journey. We will use our imagination to take us back nearly two thousand years. Imagine yourself standing just inside the gate of Bethlehem. Look around and see that the narrow streets are almost deserted, for it is well past midnight.

But look! Before us, just entering the city, is a group of shepherds. Look how excited they seem—how full of wonder they appear! They hurry along as if led by some invisible guide, and now we join them, sharing in their sense of awe. We stop at the small entrance of a grotto cave set in a steep hillside. It is a stable!

A man quietly comes forth from the cave and greets the shepherds. The man is Joseph. With a smile he bids the shepherds to enter the stable. We follow the shepherds into the cave. In the stable we see a young woman seated near the manger. Joseph calls her Mary. How lovely she looks. Her face is soft and glowing.

Mary beckons the shepherds to come closer, and with them we crowd around the manger. There, wrapped in bands of cloth, lying on the straw, is a newborn baby. Mary and Joseph tell us that his name is Jesus: he is to be the Savior of the world. Like no other baby, Jesus is surrounded by a radiance of light which the angels seem to weave.

The shepherds kneel in rapture. With a rush of feelings, we, too, fall to our knees; we sense a warmth in our hearts. The feeling of love fills our whole being—love for the Child, love for Mary and Joseph, love for the shepherds, love for God—and love for all the world!

The joyous peace of heaven enfolds us and we hear the sound of angels singing, "Glory to God in the highest and peace to all people on earth. Peace! Christ is born! Christ is born!"

Have everyone sit quietly for a few minutes, then ask them to slowly open their eyes. Light the white candle in the middle of the Advent wreath.

Action Response

Invite the children to come forward, one at a time, to take a piece of straw from the basket, and to place it in the manger.

Closing Prayer

Advent Waits
Mayla Powers

The Advent waiting now is done
And Mary has her little Son;
For him our hearts are open wide—
And so begins the Christmastide!

For twelve more days—
each Holy Night—
his star and angels bring us light.

Closing Song

Soon and Very Soon, or another song of your choosing

Receiving Christmas Cards

Goal

To use Christmas cards as an opportunity to pray for people who send holiday greetings.

Gather

- Desk or table
- Ribbon (green or red)
- Pens
- Matches
- Bible(s)
- Christmas cards (as they are received)
- Hole punch
- Scissors
- Candle
- Basket

Guide

This is an excellent activity for students to do at home with their families, but you can also do this in the classroom by having the children bring in any Christmas cards they receive prior to the holidays.

Christmas is a wonderful time to remember family and friends in many ways, and provides an occasion to share greetings with people near and far. Sending and receiving Christmas cards also offers an opportunity to remember people in prayer. In this activity, the class will set aside a special time to pray for each person who sends a holiday card.

Place a candle on a classroom or kitchen table as a symbol of Jesus' presence during this prayer experience. Place ribbon, scissors, pens, and a hole punch in a basket and set it on the table, too. Take each card as it arrives, and write a prayer on the inside of the card. Repeat the words silently or out loud. Or, offer a prayer such as this:

God, Source of Love, show your care and goodness to (name). Fill (name)'s heart and mind with good things and be an abundant source of strength for (his or her) life. We ask this in the name of Jesus, the Lord, who came as our Savior. Amen.

Punch a hole in the upper left corner of the first card. Cut a twelve-inch piece of ribbon and thread it through the card, tying it in a bow. You can then join the cards together by stringing a long piece of ribbon through a loop of each bow, and tying a small knot at each loop to hold it in place. Then hang the cards where they can be seen. Or, simply collect the cards in a nice basket or Christmas bowl.

As additional greetings arrive, repeat the process of saying a prayer and adding the card to the collection. Keep the cards displayed in a prominent place as a reminder of the communion of family and friends who share in the celebration of the birth of Christ.

Sharing Christmas Music

Goal

To share the Christmas story through Scripture and song.

Gather

- Music for selected songs
- Bible(s)
- Paper
- Duplicating equipment

Guide

For many people, a highlight of Christmas is singing the carols of the season. As a unique approach to celebrating the birth of Christ, tell the Christmas story through Scripture and song.

The carols suggested here can be sung as solos, by a choir, or by everyone. If you have children who play an instrument, feature them playing selections on piano, guitar, brass, percussion, string, or woodwind instruments—whatever the talents of your group allow. Alternate singing the carols with instrumental performances for a pleasing variety.

This is a great event for several classes to prepare together for the parish, the school, or for a small group of parents and others in the local community. It also works well as a family night activity or a theme for a school assembly.

Opening Song

O Come, All Ye Faithful

Call to Worship

Reader   Sing for joy, O heavens, and exult, O earth; break forth, O mountains, into singing! For the Lord has comforted his people, and will have compassion on his suffering ones. (Isaiah 49:13)

ALL	I will be glad and exult in you; I will sing praise to your name most high. (Psalm 9:2)
Reader	Sing and rejoice, O daughter of Zion; for lo, I will come and dwell in your midst, says the Lord. (Zechariah 2:10)
ALL	Glory to God in the highest heaven, and on earth peace among those whom he favors. (Luke 2:14)

Scripture Reading *Luke 2:1, 3–5*

In those days a decree went out from Emperor Augustus that all the world should be registered. All went to their own towns to be registered. Joseph also went from the town of Nazareth in Galilee to Judea, to the city of David called Bethlehem, because he was descended from the house and family of David. He went to be registered with Mary, to whom he was engaged and who was expecting a child.

Carol

O Little Town Of Bethlehem

Scripture Reading *Luke 2:6–7*

While they were there, the time came for her to deliver her child. And she gave birth to her firstborn son and wrapped him in bands of cloth, and laid him in a manger, because there was no place for them in the inn.

Carol

Silent Night or *O Holy Night*

Scripture Reading *Luke 2:8–9*

And in that region there were shepherds, keeping watch over their flock by night.

Carol

While Shepherds Watched Their Flock By Night

Scripture Reading *Luke 2:10–12*

But the angel said to them, "Do not be afraid; for see—I am bringing you good news of great joy for all the people: to you is born this day in the city of David a Savior, who is the Messiah, the Lord. This will be a sign for you: you will find a child wrapped in bands of cloth and lying in a manger."

Carol

The First Noel

Scripture Reading   *Luke 2:13–14*

And suddenly there was with the angel a multitude of the heavenly host, praising God and saying, "Glory to God in the highest heaven, and on earth peace among those whom he favors!"

Carol

Angels We Have Heard on High

Scripture Reading   *Luke 2:15–17*

When the angels had left them and gone into heaven, the shepherds said to one another, "Let us go now to Bethlehem and see this thing that has taken place, which the Lord has made known to us." So they went with haste and found Mary and Joseph, and the child lying in the manger. When they saw this, they made known what had been told them about this child.

Carol

Away in a Manger

Scripture Reading   *Matthew 2:1–2,11*

Wise men from the East came to Jerusalem, asking, "Where is the child who has been born king of the Jews? For we observed his star, and have come to pay him homage." On entering the house, they saw the child with Mary his mother; and they knelt down and paid him homage. Then, opening their treasure chests, they offered him gifts of gold, frankincense, and myrrh.

Carol

We Three Kings

Closing Prayer

God of all creation, thank you for the great gift of your son, Jesus. Let us always try to live according to his example. All through the year, we promise to share the love of Jesus with our family, friends, and all we meet.

Closing Song

Joy to the World

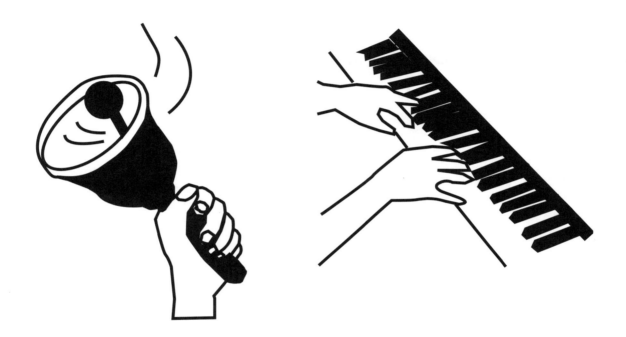

Experiencing Epiphany Traditions

Goal

To explore Epiphany traditions through participation in an event that includes prayer, education, and activity.

Gather

- Bible(s)
- Materials vary with selected activities

Guide

Celebrate the Epiphany by experiencing some of the varied traditions that mark this sacred feast. This prayer lesson begins with a gathering, branches off into activity time, then calls everyone back together to conclude with an Epiphany procession. You can choose one or more of the following activities for your class, or adapt this prayer lesson to include several classes. These activities can also be used for a parish or school event that includes several grade levels.

Begin by gathering everyone together for a welcome, opening song, and brief explanation of the event. Continue the event by proceeding to individual classrooms, or tables within a larger area, for activity time. Five activities are provided, however, more or less may be used depending on the size of the crowd. Include group as well as individual projects. Displays of Epiphany-related art may also be shared.

At the conclusion of the activity time, form a procession, led by a star banner or other Epiphany symbol. Process through the hall, classrooms, or wherever appropriate for your group.

Following prayer, if time and resources allow, invite the participants to nurture body and spirit at a Twelfth Night buffet featuring twelve different desserts or dishes. Be sure to include a king's cake.

Words of Welcome

Leader   We gather together today to celebrate the feast of the Epiphany, the day that marks the visit of the wise men to the Christ Child. As the wise men brought gifts of gold, frankincense, and myrrh, let us offer the baby the gift of our time, talent, and love for one another.

Opening Song   Choose from one of the following:

The First Noel, What Child Is This? or *We Three Kings*

Overview and Dismissal

The leader or facilitator for the event should give a brief overview of the Epiphany. Next, explain the procedure for the activities, prayer, and refreshments that will take place during the rest of the event. Finally, direct everyone to the appropriate areas for the activity time.

Activities

Epiphany Poems
Materials

Paper, 8 1/2" x 11"; pens or pencils.
Optional: construction paper; stapler and staples.

Advance Preparation

- Copy the samples shown on a large sheet of paper to display as examples.
- Optional: prepare an Epiphany booklet in which the poems of the group will be copied. Use a sheet of construction paper as the cover, and several pieces of white paper on the inside. Fold the booklet in half. Staple it in several places on the center crease. Write a title on the cover, such as "An Epiphany Journey Book."

Method

Distribute a piece of paper and a pen or pencil to each person. Share the poetry samples printed below and invite them to create their own Epiphany writings.

Two Word Poems

Each line should have only two words. Write as many lines as desired.

Holy star
Ever leading
Shine today.

Acrostic Poems

Use one word as the outline and write words which begin with each of its letters.

Salvation
Twinkling
Advent
Revelation

Couplets

Write two lines that rhyme.

The star shone bright
That holy night.

Cinquain

Create a five line poem that follows this pattern:

Line One: A one-word title that is the subject of the poem
Line Two: Two words that describe line one
Line Three: Three action words
Line Four: Four words that express a feeling about the subject.
Line Five: A synonym for line one.

Epiphany
Wondrous journey
Seeking, searching, finding
God's love swaddling clothed
Revelation

Prepositional Phrase Poetry

Use any prepositional phrases to start each line of a poetic thought.

From the Father
By the Spirit
Through the Son
Of the virgin
With his blessing
To the world.

Optional: *When everyone has written at least one Epiphany poem, collect each paper and copy it into the Epiphany booklet. These can be read at the closing prayer service if time allows. Or, individual poems can be hung up in the classroom.*

Star Banner

Materials

Fabric for banner; gold, white, and/or blue material for stars; star patterns; pens or permanent markers; fabric glue or fusible fabric bond; rod on which to hang the banner.

Advance Preparation

• Prepare the banner background by hemming and pressing the fabric. Make a channel at the top of the banner to slide in the rod.

• Copy star patterns.

Method

Invite the participants to choose a star pattern or to make one on scrap paper. (Use small and large stars!) Select a piece of star material and have each person trace their pattern on it. Be sure to put the stars as close together as possible on the fabric so that it is used efficiently. Even small triangles and dots can be bonded to the background. Use the scraps.

Ask each person to write his or her name or a wish for the new year on their cloth star. When everyone has finished writing, gather the stars together and arrange them on the banner. Place them creatively, putting large stars near smaller ones, and mixing up the colors. Carefully glue each star down. (If you choose to use fusible fabric bond, have an iron and board handy—and watch out for little ones getting too close to the hot iron!)

When all of the stars have been placed on the banner, slide the rod through the top channel. One person on each side can then carry the banner in the closing procession.

Wise Men

Materials

Construction paper; wrapping and foil paper; scissors; crayons or markers; glue; trims.

Method

Make stand-up wise men that are formed in two parts. Begin with the body. Cut paper into squares. Fold each piece in half. Cut a slit to the right and left hand sides of the top edges. Form the head by cutting a rectangle of paper proportionate to the size of the body. It should be half as wide as the colored squares. Make two slits in the head at the bottom edge.

Using markers, draw the face on the small piece of paper. Add trims and scraps of wrapping and foil paper to decorate the two pieces. Mount the faces by pushing the slits at the bottom of the rectangles over the slits at the top of the squares. Stand up the wise men.

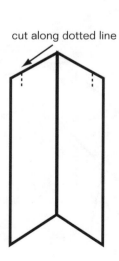

cut along dotted line

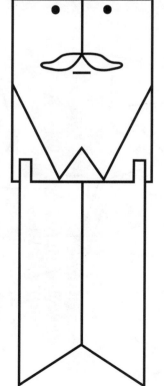

Create a Crown

Materials

Posterboard; scissors; crown patterns; glue; construction paper; stickers, glitter, and/or sequins; staplers and staples.

Advance Preparation

• Cut the posterboard into long, narrow strips, approximately 24" long x 4" wide.

Method

Have each person choose a posterboard strip. Using a pattern or freehand, cut a decorative edge along the top of the posterboard strip. Include scallops, points, or other interesting shapes. Decorate the crown using jewels cut from different colored pieces of construction paper, along with stickers, glitter, or sequins.

After measuring the crown to fit the person's head, staple the ends of the crown together. Wear it majestically during the rest of the event.

cut along dotted line

Woven Star

Materials

Construction paper; star pattern; scissors; paper cutter; ribbon; string.

Advance Preparation

• Cut the construction paper into squares.

• Cut paper and ribbon into strips for weaving.

Method

Choose a construction paper square. Fold the square in half and place a folded star pattern on top of it. Match the edges. Trace the pattern carefully. Cut out the star and cut slits where lines are indicated on the pattern. Unfold the star.

Choose six or seven strips to weave in and out of the slits. Ribbon may be woven along with paper strips. If the strips are wide, the design may only take three, four or five pieces. Weave the strip under and over, starting each one just the opposite of the previous strip. For example, if the first strip starts over, under, over, then the next strip goes under, over, under. It is easiest to start in the middle.

Put a small amount of glue at the top of the woven strip to keep it in place. Continue weaving until the design is completed. Streamers of paper or ribbon may be attached to the bottom of the star. Punch a hole in the top of the star with a pencil point or scissor blade. Tie on string to allow the star to hang.

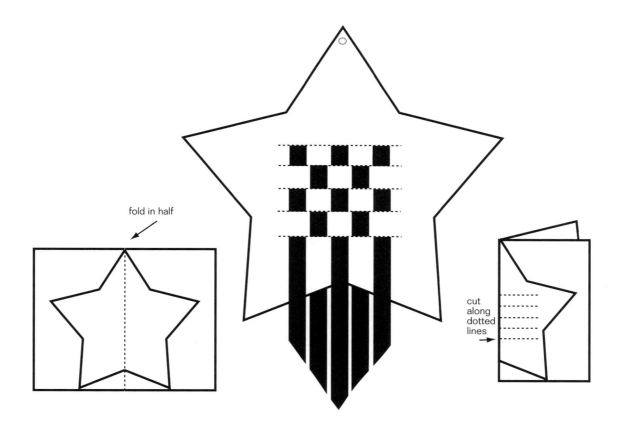

fold in half

cut along dotted lines

When the group has finished with the activities, have everyone gather to form a procession, with the star banner in the lead. Process through the parish or school hall or through several classrooms or through the church or wherever convenient to your situation. Participants can sing a song as they march, such as "I Am the Light of the World," "We Three Kings," or another song of your choosing.

Bring the procession to close as all gather around a prayer table or the church altar for a closing prayer service.

Litany of Repentance

Leader	Let us pray…God of all, we often take the wrong path on our journey through life.
ALL	Lord, have mercy on us.
Leader	Gracious God, grant us humility, knowing that we fall short of the ideal.
ALL	Lord, have mercy on us.
Leader	Almighty God, grant us persistence, knowing we are easily discouraged.
ALL	Lord, have mercy on us.
Leader	God of all wisdom, grant us clear vision, knowing we are often confused.
ALL	Lord, have mercy on us.
Leader	God of power and might, grant us strength, knowing we often yield to pressure.
ALL	Lord, have mercy on us.
Leader	God who is all wise, grant us wisdom, knowing we often make foolish choices.
ALL	Lord, have mercy on us.
Leader	Merciful God, grant us pardon, knowing we have all sinned.
ALL	Lord, have mercy on us.
Leader	Look down on us, Lord, your pilgrim people, and accept the gifts we offer you today. Thank you for the great gift of Jesus. "For God so loved the world that he gave his only Son, so everyone who believes in him may not perish but have eternal life." (John 3:16)

Carol

Angels from the Realms of Glory

Scripture Reading   *Matthew 2:7–12*

Then Herod secretly called for the wise men and learned from them the exact time when the star had appeared. Then he sent them to Bethlehem, saying, "Go and search diligently for the child; and when you have found him, bring me word so that I may also go and pay him homage."

When they had heard the king, they set out; and there, ahead of them, went the star that they had seen at its rising, until it stopped over the place where the child was. When they saw that the star had stopped, they were overwhelmed with joy. On entering the house, they saw the child with Mary his mother; and they knelt down and paid him homage. Then, opening their treasure chests, they offered him gifts of gold, frankincense, and myrrh. And having been warned in a dream not to return to Herod, they left for their own country by another road.

Take a few moments for all to reflect quietly on the reading.

Closing Prayer

The light is given at Christmas and at the Epiphany.
Help us, O Lord, to see things in the light of what you have done…
    in the light of the incarnation…
    in the light of healing…
    in the ministry of teaching…
    in the ministry of serving…
    in the light of new life.
Amen.

Closing Song

We Three Kings

Twelfth Night Buffet

If time and resources allow, plan a Twelfth Night buffet to conclude this Epiphany experience. You might want to feature twelve different desserts or dishes, including a king's cake.

King's Cake

You will need:

1 1/4 cup butter or margarine, softened

2 3/4 cups sugar

5 eggs

1 tablespoon fresh lemon juice

3 cups flour

1 teaspoon baking powder

1/4 teaspoon salt

1 cup evaporated milk

2 teaspoons grated lemon peel

1 large dried bean or pea

candy gumdrops

For glaze

1/3 cup butter or margarine

2 cups powdered sugar

2-3 tablespoons fresh lemon juice

hot water (as needed)

Method

Heat the oven to 350 degrees.

Combine butter or margarine, sugar, eggs, and lemon juice in a large mixing bowl on low speed for one minute, scraping the bowl constantly. Beat five minutes on high speed. Mix in flour, baking powder, and salt alternately with the milk on low speed. Add lemon peel and mix to blend. Stir in the dried bean.

Pour the batter into a greased and floured tube pan. Bake for one hour and fifteen minutes. Cool the cake in the pan for twenty minutes. Remove it from the pan and allow it to cool completely.

Make the glaze by melting one-third cup butter or margarine, and stirring in two cups powdered sugar and the lemon juice. Beat until smooth. Add one tablespoon of hot water at a time until the mixture reaches the desired consistency. Pour over the cake.

Decorate the cake with candy gum drops of various colors and sizes to represent jewels.

Responding with Gifts

Goal

To make "gift bags" to be used in an Epiphany prayer service celebrating all God's gifts.

Gather

- Paper lunch bags or grocery bags
- Hole punches
- Tape
- Scissors
- Gift wrap
- Candle
- Table
- Tape or CD player
- Cassette tape or CD of tranquil background music
- Bible(s)
- Yarn
- Magazines
- Glue sticks
- Ribbon
- Matches
- Tablecloth

Advance Preparation

- Place the table in the center or the front of the room.
- Cover the table with a cloth and arrange the candle, matches, and Bible on it.

Guide

The feast of Epiphany, January 6, is a time to celebrate that Jesus was, is, and continues to be God's gift of salvation for the world. The word "epiphany," which means "manifestation," reminds us that Christ is God's gift of grace to all humanity.

The three kings—also called magi or wise men—brought gifts to the greatest Gift the world has ever experienced. To honor this memory, Epiphany is a time of gift-giving in many parts of the Christian world.

On January 6, or a day close to this date, reflect on God's gift of the Savior and respond in prayer and praise. Invite each student to create a gift bag to use in an Epiphany prayer service. Begin by distributing a paper bag to each person. Place hole punches, heavy yarn, and tape within reach of the children. Demonstrate how to punch two holes on each side of the top of the sack. To create handles, string heavy yarn through each set of holes and tie it inside of the bag. Reinforce the holes with tape. Provide time for the participants to complete this process.

Invite each student to think of a personal gift or talent to share with others. For example, a person with a beautiful voice could sing a song during a prayer service; someone good in science could help a student who has trouble with the subject; and a confident reader could share stories with younger or older people.

Distribute magazines and scissors and direct the group to find pictures and words to describe their gifts. Instruct the group to cut out the illustrations and to glue them to the outside of their bags. Once the activity is completed, invite the participants to place their gift bags on the floor around the prayer table and to gather for prayer.

Opening Song

Gather Us In or another song of your choosing.

Opening Prayer

Reader	The person who gives with kindness shall live on the Lord's holy mountain.
ALL	The person who gives with kindness shall live on the Lord's holy mountain.
Reader	Walk blamelessly and do justice; fill your heart with truth and slander not with your tongue.
ALL	The person who gives with kindness shall live on the Lord's holy mountain.
Reader	Harm no one in word or action, give to those in need, giving from your plenty.
ALL	The person who gives with kindness shall live on the Lord's holy mountain.
Reader	Lend without repayment, give without your neighbor's knowledge, accept no bribes against the innocent.
ALL	The person who gives with kindness shall live on the Lord's holy mountain.

Scripture Readings

Matthew 2:1–12

In the time of King Herod, after Jesus was born in Bethlehem of Judea, wise men from the East came to Jerusalem, asking, "Where is the child who has been born king of the Jews? For we observed his star at its rising, and have come to pay him homage."

When King Herod heard this, he was frightened, and all Jerusalem with him; and calling together all the chief priests and scribes of the people, he inquired of them where the Messiah was to be born. They told him, "In Bethlehem of Judea; for so it has been written by the prophet: 'And you, Bethlehem, in the land of Judah, are by no means least among the rulers of Judah; for from you shall come a ruler who is to shepherd my people Israel.'"

Then Herod secretly called for the wise men and learned from them the exact time when the star had appeared. Then he sent them to Bethlehem, saying, "Go and search diligently for the child; and when you have found him, bring me word so that I may also go and pay him homage."

When they had heard the king, they set out; and there, ahead of them, went the star that they had seen at its rising, until it stopped over the place where the child was. When they saw that the star had stopped, they were overwhelmed with joy. On entering the house, they saw the child with Mary his mother; and they knelt down and paid him homage. Then, opening their treasure chests they offered him gifts of gold, frankincense, and myrrh. And having been warned in a dream not to return to Herod, they left for their own country by another road.

Colossians 3:12–17

Because you are God's chosen ones, holy and beloved, clothe yourselves with heartfelt mercy, with kindness, humility, meekness, and patience. Bear with one another; forgive whatever grievances you have against one another. Forgive as the Lord has forgiven you. Over all these virtues put on love, which binds the rest together and makes them perfect. Christ's peace must reign in your hearts, since as members of the one body you have been called to that peace.

Dedicate yourselves to thankfulness. Let the word of Christ, rich as it is, dwell in you. In wisdom made perfect, instruct one another. Sing gratefully to God from your hearts. Whatever you do, whether in speech or action, do it in the name of the Lord Jesus.

Action Response

Invite the participants to remember the gifts that they depicted on their bags. Remind the group that these God-given gifts are to be shared with God's people. Invite each person to take a few moments to reflect on a way that his or her gift can be shared with others.

Distribute the wrapping paper squares, ribbon, pens, and hole punches. Direct the students to punch a hole in the top of the square and to tie a piece of ribbon through it. It should resemble a gift tag. Tell the children to write on the tags ways that they will share their gifts.

Light the candle and play reflective background music. After a few moments of silence, invite the participants to come forward, one at a time, to attach the tag to their bag. Remind the group that this action symbolizes a willingness to share their gifts with others, just as God shared his son, Jesus, with us.

As each tag is placed on a bag, repeat a prayer, such as this:

Bless this gift we bring you today. May it be for us a reminder of your goodness.

Closing Prayer

Almighty God, we have gathered here today to give thanks for the gift of your son, Jesus Christ. In response to the gift of his coming among us through your all-powerful love, we share our talents and gifts with others.

We promise to love with a deeper heart and to see with a clearer vision. We pray this in the name of Jesus, the everlasting gift of life. Amen.

Closing Song

Blest Are They or another song of your choosing.

Observing Ash Wednesday

Goal

To use an Ash Wednesday litany as a way to help students see Lent as a time to feast as well as a time to fast.

Gather

- Ash Wednesday litany
- Duplicating equipment
- Paper
- Bible(s)

Advance Preparation

- Make a copy of the Ash Wednesday litany for everyone in the class.

Guide

Traditionally, Lent is known as a season of "giving things up." Usually, that means letting go of something we enjoy. The true goal of the lenten season, however, is to rid ourselves of the sin that encumbers us so we can fully embrace our God.

Use the following litany on Ash Wednesday to challenge students to see Lent both as a time to fast and as a time to feast.

Ash Wednesday Litany

Reader   Lent is a time of fasting, of cleansing ourselves from sin.

ALL   We seek to rid ourselves of all that would weigh us down.

Reader   Lent is also a time of feasting, a time of celebrating the message of God's goodness.

ALL   We long to experience God's joy, which lifts us up.

Reader   During Lent, let us fast from judging others and emphasizing our differences.

ALL   Instead, we will feast on Christ's presence dwelling in others.

Reader   Let us feast on the unity found in God's universe.

ALL   We will not indulge in thoughts that defeat us.

Reader   Fast from thoughts of illness, discontent, and anger.

ALL   We will choose to feast on God's healing power and our gratitude!

Reader   Fast from pessimism and worry; feast on optimism and trust.

ALL   We will hold ourselves from complaining and from focusing on the negative; we will feast on appreciation and affirmation.

Reader   Refuse to take in stress; feast on moments of prayerful serenity.

ALL   Our hearts will reject discouragement, but we will open our lives to hope.

Reader   This lenten season, turn toward God and fast from self-centeredness.

ALL   We will find God as we feast on prayer and compassion. Amen.

God's grace
prayerful serenity
God's healing power
hope patience and trust
celebrate the message
of God's goodness

worry jealousy
anger impatience pride
stress complaining

Tasting Lenten Traditions

Goal

To explore the symbolism of foods associated with the seasons of Lent and Easter.

Gather

- Bible(s)
- Supplies will vary with activities selected.

Guide

Easter is considered a "moveable feast," which means the date for the holiday changes each year. Easter falls on the first Sunday after the first full moon following the vernal equinox—the date in spring when the days and nights are of equal length, usually March 21. Lent begins forty days before Easter, excluding Sundays. (Sundays are not included in the forty days since they are considered "feast" days.)

Help students gain a better understanding of Lent and Easter by arranging a "moveable feast." Share special foods and significant information in several different settings. The group may move to different rooms within a church or school or to various homes. At each site, explain an important part of Lent and Easter, feature a symbolic food, and offer a prayer.

Shrove Tuesday

Food: *Pancakes*
Theme: *History of custom*

Shrove Tuesday is the last day to feast before Lent begins. This day is also known as Mardi Gras, which means "fat Tuesday." This is a day of celebration before the forty-day period of penitence. It is a time to use up meat, eggs, butter, and other perishables that will not last through Lent. Rich pastries and fried foods are often served on Shrove Tuesday.

Provide pancakes or pastries and explore some of the interesting ways this day is celebrated around the world. Offer a prayer of thanks for the richness of God's goodness.

Ash Wednesday

Food: *Fasting*
Theme: *Hunger project*

On Ash Wednesday, the first day of Lent, many people pray and fast. The foreheads of believers are marked with ashes in the shape of a cross as a sign of repentance and humility.

There should be no food to taste at this station. Provide handouts with information about the church's teaching on fasting and abstinence during Lent. Also provide materials about hunger projects within the community. Consider asking for an offering of money or canned goods for a food bank.

Pray that God will fill the physical, emotional, and spiritual hungers in people's lives.

Palm Sunday

Food: *Pretzels*
Theme: *Prayer*

On Palm Sunday, the crowds greeted Jesus with palm branches as he entered Jerusalem. This day marks the beginning of Holy Week.

In the fifth century, Roman monks baked pretzels as reminders of the prayerful season. The simple dough made from flour, salt, and water was shaped to represent arms crossed in prayer. In some European countries, such as Germany and Austria, pretzels are hung from palm branches on Palm Sunday.

Make pretzel dough from scratch, prepare frozen soft pretzels, or purchase packages of pretzel twists and serve them at this station. This would be a good time to share lessons on prayer, to explain various types of prayers, and to offer lenten prayerbooks and stations of the cross booklets.

Conclude this activity by inviting the participants to cross their arms over their chests—in the shape of a pretzel—and to thank God for the opportunity to speak to him in prayer.

Holy Thursday

Food: *Unleavened bread*
Theme: *Eucharist*

When Jesus and his disciples gathered to share the Passover meal in the upper room, they would have eaten unleavened bread. (Look up Exodus 12 in your Bible for the story of the Passover.)

Holy Thursday is also called "Maundy" Thursday, a word that comes from *mandatum,* Latin for commandment. At the Last Supper, Jesus gave the disciples two commandments: to love one another and to remember his sacrifice through the sacrament of the Eucharist.

Share unleavened bread in a simple communion service. Explain other commemorative celebrations such as a Passover seder observance or an agape meal (this is a non-sacramental meal shared in the spirit of Christian love).

Provide an opportunity for the students to offer prayers of gratitude to God for Jesus' willingness to be "broken" in their place.

Good Friday

Food: *Hot cross buns*
Theme: *Worship*

Some historians believe that Good Friday was originally known as "God's Friday." The special name for the day recognizes that what God did on this day was indeed good.

Hot cross buns have been popular for centuries as a lenten food. The buns have raisins and citron in the dough and a cross of white icing on the top. Have a recipe and supplies ready to make hot cross buns or purchase the treats at a bakery or supermarket. Offer hot cross buns and something to drink at this station.

Invite participants to add a word or a phrase to a prayer to describe the importance of Jesus' cross in their lives.

Holy Saturday

Food: *Hard-boiled eggs*
Theme: *Food baskets for shut-ins*

In some cultures, it is a custom to prepare a basket of food on Holy Saturday morning and to present it at church for a special blessing. The foods in the basket are eaten at a family celebration later that night or on Easter Sunday.

Traditional items to include in the baskets are:

• Colored eggs: signify new life;
• Molded butter or cake in the shape of a lamb: represents Jesus as the sacrificial lamb;
• Loaf of bread: depicts the staff of life;

• Salt: illustrates the symbol of truth;
• Horseradish: highlights the bitter gall given to quench Christ's thirst;
• Ham: symbolizes Christ conquering the old laws.

Share the symbolism of the foods with the students and prepare food baskets to deliver to families and shut-ins. Say a prayer as the ingredients are placed in the basket, asking God to bless the person who will receive the gift.

Easter

Food: *Sampling of traditional foods*
Theme: *Family customs and recipes*

Plan to end the "moveable feast" with a time of prayer or a way to summarize the information that was shared at the various stations. In addition to the "tastes" of the season, try organizing a more elaborate event to share actual foods or recipes that are part of family Lent and Easter traditions.

Offer a prayer of praise for God's gift of new life through Jesus Christ.

Writing Prayer Poems

Goal

To write prayer poems for use in a lenten booklet.

Gather

- Bible(s)
- Journal or paper
- Pens

Guide

Writing activities, especially poetry, can be used to help people discover creative ways to express their thoughts and feelings. During the seasons of Lent and Easter, individual and group prayer can be enhanced by incorporating creative writing experiences into the prayers.

Offer the opportunity to use poetry as a way to reflect, remember, and respond before, during, or after classes, events, or services. Compile individual or group prayer booklets to use during the special days of Lent and Easter.

For use as an at-home project, print the instructions in a bulletin, newsletter, or on a take-home sheet, and suggest ways for people of all ages—children, youth, and adults—to write personal prayer poems related to the events of Jesus' ministry and mission.

Experiment with different poetry patterns and themes. Some examples follow.

Rhymes

Write a traditional four-line poem in which every other line rhymes. Use one of the lenten gospel stories, such as Lazarus being raised from the dead or the woman at the well, as a theme. Incorporate situations which prevent people from attaining and maintaining a spiritual relationship with God.

Jesus called Lazarus forth from the tomb
And brought him into the light.
We too want to come out of darkness and sin
By doing what's good and what's right.

Quick Couplets

A quick couplet contains two lines with three syllables in each line, such as:

Line One: Jesus' word
Line Two: Must be heard!

Line One: Let me live
Line Two: To forgive.

Cinquain

A cinquain poem contains five lines and is based on the following formula:

Line one: *a one-word noun*
Line two: *two adjectives that describe the noun*
Line three: *three "ing" words that describe the noun*
Line four: *four words that express a feeling about the noun*
Line five: *one word that is a synonym for the noun*

Jesus
Divine, human
Loving, sharing, giving
King of my life
Savior

Diamond Poem

Try a five-line, diamond-shaped poem as a way to think about Jesus' betrayal.

Line one: *one word which is an opposite of line five*
Line two: *two words which describe line one*
Line three: *three words which resolve the conflict*
Line four: *two words which describe line five*
Line five: *one word which is an opposite of line one*

Betrayal
Deception, dishonesty
Conscience, sincerity, trust
Faithful, steadfast
Loyalty

Free Verse

Express emotions by writing free verse, a style of poetry without a pattern of rhyme and rhythm. This example uses images related to the events of Good Friday.

Jesus, gentle teacher,
You died for us
So that we might live.

On this holy day
We remember your great love for us
And praise your name
Forever.

Shape Poems

Write the words of a poem in the shape of a symbol of new life, such as a butterfly or a flower.

Jesus,
from the dark
tomb you rose
into new life. Just
as the butterfly comes
out of the cocoon
into beauty and
awe.

Acrostic

An acrostic poem uses the letters of a word to start words that describe or relate to that particular word. Here is an example using the word "Easter."

Easter
Almighty
Savior
Triumphant
Everlasting
Resurrection

Praising with Palms

Goal

To create "palm" palms and praise prayers for use in a parade or procession

Gather

- Bible(s)
- Scissors
- Glue
- Cardboard rolls from hangers or paper towel tubes
- Green construction paper
- Pens or markers
- Tape

Guide

Imagine the excitement as Jesus entered Jerusalem on Palm Sunday! People of all ages proclaimed him their king. Paths were strewn with garments as gestures of welcome. Psalms of praise were shouted. Palm branches were waved as symbols of victory.

Recreate some of the exhilaration of this scene by constructing unique "palm" palms, writing prayers of praise, and participating in a Palm Sunday parade or procession. Begin this lesson by reading a Scripture passage containing the Palm Sunday story such as Matthew 21:1–11, Mark 11:1–11, Luke 19:28–40, or John 12:12–19.

Distribute the supplies to the class, giving each child a piece of green construction paper, a cardboard roll, and a pen or marker. Ask the children to place one of their hands, palm down, on the construction paper. Trace around the hand, then cut out the hand shapes to use as the palm leaves.

Write prayers of praise on the palms, such as:

Jesus, you are the king of my life.

Thank you, God, for the gift of your son.

Praise to God, our heavenly father!

Attach the palm leaves to the cardboard rolls with glue or tape. Use the palm branches and the prayers during a Palm Sunday processional, as part of a class activity, for a parade through the neighborhood, or on a visit to a retirement community.

Connecting the Sevens

Goal

To make a correlation between the seven corporal works of mercy and the seven last words of Jesus, and to emphasize these themes in lenten prayer and practice.

Gather

- Purple candles (seven) and holders
- Table
- Baskets (seven large ones)
- Index cards, 3" x 5"
- Crayons or markers
- List of seven last words of Jesus
- List of corporal works of mercy
- Information on social justice projects

- Matches
- Tablecloth
- Bible(s)
- Paper, 8 1/2" x 11"
- Duplicating equipment

Advance Preparation

- Create a prayer table in the center or off to the side of a room. Cover the table with a cloth and set seven purple candles on it. Place seven baskets on the floor.
- Prepare a 3" x 5" index card for each student. Print one of the seven last words on one side of each card.
- Research seven service projects for the students to participate in. Inform them of the projects in advance so they can collect and bring in the appropriate items for each prayer service.

Guide

This prayer lesson offers an opportunity to combine the seven last words of Jesus with the seven corporal works of mercy. Students will use this theme to explore a social justice emphasis in their prayer and spiritual practice throughout the season of Lent.

Explain that during Lent, beginning the week of Ash Wednesday, the group will reflect on Jesus' statements from the cross. (These seven "words" are actually phrases selected from the passion accounts of the four gospels.) Read the seven verses aloud.

Seven Last Words of Jesus

1. "Father, forgive them; for they do not know what they are doing." Luke 23:34

2. "Father, into your hands I commend my spirit." Luke 23:46

3. "I am thirsty." John 19:28

4. "It is finished." John 19:30

5. "My God, my God, why have you forsaken me?" Matthew 27:46; Mark 15:34

6. "Truly, I tell you, today you will be with me in Paradise." Luke 23:43

7. "Woman, here is your son!...Here is your mother." John 19:26, 27

Distribute an index card with one of these phrases to each child. Place sheets of paper and crayons or markers within sharing distance of the students. Invite them to draw a picture of the "word" they received.

When the drawings are completed, assemble the children in a line, ordered numerically according to their card. Then have the children sit down. Ask all of the children with the first word to stand up with their drawing and to face the rest of the group. Read the phrase and invite each child to take a turn to talk about his or her picture of the verse. When everyone in the first group has had an opportunity to share, have them sit down and continue with the next group until all seven groups have participated. Display the drawings on the prayer table, or hang them up.

When this part of the project is completed, distribute a list of the corporal works of mercy. Since the season of Lent offers an opportunity for service, explain that each of Jesus' words from the cross will be matched with one of the works of mercy. Read the list aloud.

Corporal Works of Mercy

Clothe the naked.
Shelter the homeless.
Visit the imprisoned.
Feed the hungry.
Give drink to the thirsty.
Care for the sick.
Bury the dead.

Invite the group to suggest projects that emphasize these themes, for example: collecting clothes for children involved in a natural disaster; visiting people who are lonely; stocking a community food pantry with canned goods.

During each week of Lent, beginning on Ash Wednesday, incorporate the two themes, the seven corporal works of mercy and the seven last words of Jesus, into a prayer experience and a practical application. (You can also do the prayer experiences for all seven weeks at one time if this is more suitable for you.)

Gather the participants around the prayer table. Light one candle each week until all seven are illuminated during Holy Week. Expand or enrich the activity by singing a song or playing music that interprets the essence of each theme.

Week One

Reader   "Father, forgive them; for they do not know what they are doing."

ALL   Clothe the naked.

Light one candle

ALL   "Father, forgive them; for they do not know what they are doing." My God, so often we are the same. We act without thinking. We overlook the needs around us. Be with us as we begin this lenten season. Give us a heart for justice. We ask this in the name of Jesus, who supplies all of our needs. Amen.

Action

Ahead of time, invite the students to collect clothing items for a social service organization. Explain the project and be specific about the kind of clothing that is needed, for example: coats, socks, sweaters, and so forth. Have the students bring the articles to the prayer service, and place them in one of the large baskets. Collected items may be distributed at the end of the week or at the end of the season of Lent.

Week Two

Reader   "Woman, here is your son!… Here is your mother."

ALL   Shelter the homeless.

Light two candles.

ALL   "Woman, here is your son! Son, here is your mother." Jesus instructed John, the beloved disciple, to care for his mother, Mary. Together they created a home, a place of comfort and safety.

     Challenge us, God of all creation, to be ever mindful of our neighbor's needs. Help us to strive to make a better world for all people. Give us the gift of generosity so our hearts will be like an open door for all who enter. We pray this in the name of Jesus, our example. Amen.

Action

Invite the participants to collect personal care items, such as shampoo, soap, and toothpaste, for a homeless center and bring them to the prayer service. Place the items in one of the baskets and distribute during Lent.

Week Three

Reader   "Truly, I tell you, today you will be with me in Paradise."

ALL   Visit the imprisoned.

Light three candles.

ALL   "Truly, I tell you, today you will be with me in Paradise." Heavenly God, through the person of Jesus you taught us, do not judge, lest you be judged. Help us to remember the good works of Jesus and the way he reached out to everyone, even to those imprisoned. Move us from what is comfortable to what will challenge our faith. Help us to love the unloved. We ask this in the name of Jesus, who loves us all. Amen.

Action

Invite the group to collect Bibles, books, and magazines for people who are imprisoned. Place the resources in the third basket.

Week Four

Reader   "My God, my God, why have you forsaken me?"

ALL   Feed the hungry.

Light four candles.

ALL   "My God, my God, why have you forsaken me?" Creator God, you know the hungers of the human heart—our needs as well as our wants. You alone can fill us with overflowing grace and love. Take our hearts of stone and give us hearts of flesh. Teach us to see the hungers around us and give us the courage to make a difference. We pray this in the name of Jesus, who is the bread of life. Amen.

Action

Invite the group to bring canned goods for a local food pantry. Collect the items in the fourth basket.

Week Five

Reader   "I am thirsty."

ALL   Give drink to the thirsty.

Light five candles.

ALL   "I am thirsty." God, giver of life, your son Jesus cried in thirst to have the anguish of his soul quenched. Help us to understand that thirst comes in many forms.

Create in us a clean heart, O God. Wash away that which is unloving and help us to reach out and give drink to those who thirst. Help us to generously pour out the waters of compassion and kindness. We ask this in the name of Jesus, our living water. Amen.

Action

Collect money to help an organization that works to provide safe water in many places throughout the world. Place the offering in the fifth basket.

Week Six

Reader	"It is finished."
ALL	Care for the sick.

Light six candles.

Reader	"It is finished." So often, God, we feel sick at heart. Our world is broken. Pain and sickness surround us. Fill us with the spirit of hope that comes from Jesus. Give us the courage to heal hurts and to renew lives. Give us Jesus' sense of concern for the sick of body, mind, and spirit. Give us grace, for Jesus' sake. Amen.

Action

Write notes of cheer to people who are sick. Place the greetings in the sixth basket.

Week Seven

Reader	"Father, into your hands I commend my spirit."
ALL	Bury the dead.

Light seven candles.

ALL	"Father, into your hands I commend my spirit." You are God of both the living and the dead. You guide our every step. You know our every thought. You know the number of days allotted to us. Help us in a spirit of love and compassion to walk with those who mourn. As you meet our needs, give us the wisdom to share the needs of others. Jesus died that all may have life. Amen.

Action

Send sympathy cards or notes to people who have experienced the loss of a loved one.

Reviewing the Way of the Cross

Goal

To illustrate a cube with scenes of the Way of the Cross.

Gather

- Cross-shaped cube pattern
- Paper
- Glue or tape
- Bible(s)
- Colored pencils or fine-tipped markers
- Pencils
- Scissors
- Way of the Cross list
- Duplicating equipment (optional)

Guide

The cube is an interesting shape. When it is opened and flattened it forms the outline of a cross. During the season of Lent, a cube can be made and decorated in ways that will help the children reflect on Jesus' passion and death. For example, each square of the cube could simply be colored to suggest a feeling or mood associated with the cross and the crucifixion. Some of the colors and their symbolism might be blue for sadness, green for growth, purple for royalty, red for blood, and yellow for hope.

Another helpful activity during Lent would be to draw scenes on each square to tell the story of Jesus' passion and death.

Since one side of a cube has six squares, choose six scenes to use for this activity, such as:

1. Jesus is condemned to death.
2. Jesus takes his cross.
3. Jesus falls.
4. Simon helps Jesus carry the cross.
5. Jesus is crucified and dies.
6. Jesus is taken from the cross and laid in the tomb.

All fourteen or fifteen stations may be illustrated by using both sides of the paper and combining two of the scenes on three of the squares.

Enlarge or reduce the cross shape to the desired size. Photocopy or trace the cube pattern onto plain paper or construction paper. Cut out the cross. Draw the scenes or print the words on the squares—outside and/or inside—putting the first picture or phrase on the square that will be the top and the last illustration or idea on the square that will be the bottom.

Determine the order by folding the cross briefly and numbering each square with the number of the scene it should contain. Sketch or letter the remaining scenes in order on the other squares. Color the scenes with fine-point markers or colored pencils.

Fold each section of the cross to the center to form the cube shape. Glue or tape the tabs in place. Set the cross cube in a special place where it can be a reminder of Jesus' love.

Offer a daily prayer of thanks for the gift of salvation we received through the death and resurrection of Jesus.

Way of the Cross

1. Jesus is condemned to death.
2. Jesus takes up his cross.
3. Jesus falls the first time.
4. Jesus meets his mother, Mary.
5. Simon helps Jesus carry his cross.
6. Veronica wipes the face of Jesus.
7. Jesus falls the second time.
8. Jesus speaks to the women.
9. Jesus falls a third time.
10. Jesus is stripped of his clothes.
11. Jesus is nailed to the cross.
12. Jesus dies on the cross.
13. Jesus is taken down from the cross.
14. Jesus is buried.
15. Jesus rises from the dead.

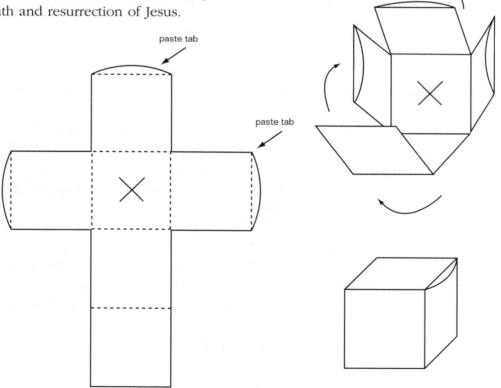

paste tab

paste tab

Symbolizing New Life

Goal

To help students celebrate the Easter theme of new life through the use of the symbol of the egg.

Gather

- Bible(s)
- Table
- Candle (white or pastel)
- Basket with Easter grass
- Eggs (hard-boiled)
- Tablecloth (white)
- Matches
- Supplies for Easter egg decorating

Advance Preparation

- Place a table in a central location and cover it with a white cloth. Arrange the basket, candle, and matches on it.
- Prepare an area for decorating the Easter eggs.

Guide

Easter eggs can be blown, hard-boiled, or preserved; butter cream, chocolate, or marshmallow; porcelain, wax, or wood; colored, dyed, or painted. Eggs are one of the most common Easter emblems because they symbolize new life.

Although an egg doesn't look alive, it contains the materials to make a living chick if it is hatched. When the shell begins to crack, out pokes a tiny beak, then a fuzzy head, and finally the small, warm body of a living bird—a miracle of new life.

In medieval times, eating eggs was prohibited during the season of Lent, so hard-boiled eggs were given as gifts to be eaten on Easter Sunday. In many cultures eggs are included in the Easter baskets that are blessed at church on Holy Saturday for use at Easter Sunday breakfasts.

To the Christian, eggs symbolically represent the Easter story. The rock hard shell represents the tomb where Jesus was buried, and the elements of new life represent Jesus' resurrection—and eternal life for the Christian!

Celebrate the symbolism of new life by decorating eggs and using them in an Easter prayer service. Choose from the half-dozen "egg decorating" options provided or use the suggestions as springboards for other projects. Once the work space is prepared and the students are assembled, discuss a variety of ways to decorate Easter eggs and demonstrate some of the techniques. Distribute one or two hard-boiled eggs to each participant and allow time for the group to experiment with different methods.

After each participant has had an opportunity to decorate one or two eggs, begin cleanup and prepare for prayer.

Egg Blowing

Provide

Eggs; large needles; containers.

Proceed

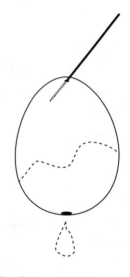

To blow out an egg, use a needle to poke a small pinhole at the narrow end of the egg and a larger hole at the opposite side. Twist the needle around inside the egg to be sure the yoke is broken. Hold the egg over a container. Blow gently but steadily through the small hole and the yolk and white will slip out the other end. Rinse and dry the egg before decorating it with paint or dyes.

Natural Egg Dyes

Provide

Eggs (raw); natural materials for dye: beet skins, onion skins, spinach leaves; string; large pan; water; stove; slotted spoon; pins; soft cloths; vegetable oil.

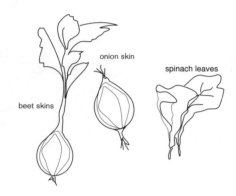

beet skins   onion skin   spinach leaves

Proceed

Wrap each egg in beet skins, onion skins, or spinach leaves. Tie the natural materials in place with string. Place the eggs in a pan and cover them with water. Boil for thirty to forty minutes and allow to cool.

Unwrap the eggs. Scratch patterns into the color with a pin. To make the colors shine, place a little cooking oil on a soft cloth and rub it over the eggs.

Fingerprint Eggs

Provide

Eggs (blown or hard-boiled); tempera paints; paper plates or sponges; wet paper towels.

Proceed

Pour a small amount of each color of paint on separate plates or sponges. Hold the egg on the ends between the thumb and index finger so it can be rotated while stamping. Dip a finger into paint, dab off the excess on a paper towel, then gently press the painted finger onto the egg. Continue until the egg is filled with fingerprints—that almost look like jellybeans!

Rubber Band Wrapped Eggs

Provide

Rubber bands, various sizes; dye; eggs (hard-boiled); pan; water; slotted spoons.

Proceed

Twist rubber bands around an egg, covering it completely. Dip the covered egg into prepared dye. The dye will seep under the bands in some areas and be blocked out in other parts. Remove the egg from the dye when it is colored. Blot dry with paper towels and remove the rubber bands. If desired, repeat the process with another color.

Sponge-painted Eggs

Provide

Eggs (blown or hard-boiled); sponges; scissors; tempera paints; containers for paints; paper towels; clip clothespins (optional).

Proceed

Put each color of paint into a separate container. Cut sponges into small pieces or shapes. If desired, clip a piece of sponge to a clothespin and use the clothespin as a handle. Dip the sponge into paint, dab off the excess, and press the sponge onto the egg. Continue until the desired pattern is achieved.

String Art Eggs

Provide

Balloons; cotton embroidery thread or thin string; white glue or liquid starch; waxed paper; water; containers; artificial flowers and leaves; narrow ribbon; tacky glue or glue gun; clothesline; scissors.

Proceed

Blow up a balloon into an egg shape—about six to eight inches, or larger if time and materials permit.

Saturate the thread or string in liquid starch or a mixture of two-thirds white glue and one-half water. Pull the thread between the first and second fingers to scrape off excess glue. Carefully wrap string around the balloon, crisscrossing threads. Continue until there is a strong "netting" covering the balloon.

Allow the balloon to dry on waxed paper in a warm, dry place. If there is a clothesline available, "eggs" may be tied to the line to dry.

When the thread is completely dry, pop the balloon with a scissor blade. Remove it through one of the larger openings.

Trim the egg with bunches of spring flowers and ribbons clustered at the top of the shape. Tie on a loop of ribbon to form a hanger. Use the eggs to make a mobile, hang as tree decorations, or arrange in a basket.

An Easter Prayer

As the participants gather for prayer, invite them to place the eggs they have made in the basket on the prayer table.

Opening Prayer

> Because of his boundless love
> He became what we are
> In order that
> He might make us what he is.
>
> —St. Irenaeus

Light the candle.

Opening Song

New Life or another song of your choosing.

Scripture Reading

(Based on Matthew 28:1–7; Mark 16:1–8; Luke 24:1–12, 36-43; John 20:1–23)

Early on Sunday morning while it was still dark, Mary Magdalene, one of the women who loved Jesus very much, went to his tomb. To her amazement, she saw that the great stone which sealed the entrance had been rolled aside. The tomb was empty!

Mary ran to find John and Peter. "They have taken away the Lord and I don't know where they have put his body," she cried. John and Peter ran to the tomb. They went inside. The linen burial cloths were there—but the Lord's body was gone!

After the disciples went away, Mary Magdalene remained outside the tomb, weeping. All at once she saw a man standing nearby. It was Jesus. But Mary did not recognize him. Jesus spoke to her, "Woman, why are you crying? Whom are you seeking?" Still Mary did not recognize him. She thought he must be the gardener. Jesus came closer. Gently he called her by name, "Mary." That was all he said, but with the utterance of her name, her eyes were opened. She knew that Jesus was alive again!

"Master!" she cried, her whole being flooded with joy! "Find my brothers," Jesus said. "Tell them that I go now to my Father and your Father; to my God and your God." When Jesus had gone, a radiant Mary hurried to the disciples. "I have seen the Lord," she cried.

That same evening the friends of Jesus were gathered together. Other followers besides Mary had seen the risen Christ. All of the witnesses told their stories about the new life of Jesus. Jesus was alive, yet most of the followers could not believe it until Jesus appeared in their midst. Jesus spoke to them, "Peace be with you." He showed them the wounds on his hands and feet. "Touch me and see for yourselves, a spirit does not have flesh and bones as I have."

For the next forty days the risen Christ taught his beloved disciples before he sent them forth to tell the world that Easter was only the beginning of new life.

Prayer Response

Reader   God is here; God is with us! It is a great time for celebration! Our praises need not be confined to old songs. Let us create new songs of praise to our God. Let us discover new ways of proclaiming God's greatness and glory.

ALL   God of new life, be praised.

Reader   The world about us reflects God's majesty. The roaring sea and all that inhabit it, the wind that bends the trees, the creatures that fill the air and land, the mountains that probe the skies, the rivers and lakes that feed our thirst, the great planets and stars that light up our night. All of these reveal God's beauty and splendor.

ALL   God of new life, be praised.

Reader   Wherever one turns, God's power is manifested, God's presence is made apparent. Let us celebrate God's presence in our world today.

ALL   God of new life, be praised.

Closing Prayer

Easter Time
Laura E. Richards

Waken, sleeping butterfly,
Burst your narrow prison.
Spread your golden wings and rise—
Christ the Lord is risen!

Spread your wings and tell the story,
How he rose, the Lord of glory!

Closing Song

New Life or another song of your choosing.

Commemorating Ascension Day

Goal

To celebrate Ascension Day by making paper crowns to illustrate that Jesus is king.

Gather

- Stickers
- Glue
- Pencils
- Stickers
- Posterboard, 2" x 22" per project
- Construction paper, various colors

- Scissors
- Rulers
- Markers

Guide

Ascension Day celebrates the fact that after God raised Jesus from the dead, God took Jesus bodily into heaven. Jesus lives in glory with God and shares his dominion over all. Scripture passages related to the story of the Ascension include Luke 24:44–53, Acts 1:1–11, Psalm 47, Psalm 93, and Ephesians 1:15–23. The church commemorates the Ascension of Jesus on the fortieth day after Easter, the Thursday after the sixth Sunday of the Easter season.

In the twenty-fourth chapter of his gospel, Luke describes the Ascension as the conclusion of a resurrection appearance of Jesus to his disciples. Jesus promised his followers that he would send the Holy Spirit to empower them to carry out the work of bringing about the kingdom of God. Although Jesus is in heaven, Jesus is present in all times and in all places. Jesus is present to us in the Word of God, in the waters of baptism, in the elements of communion, in the community of Christians, and in the heart of each believer.

Ascension Day challenges Jesus' modern-day followers to live lives that show others that Jesus is king. Explain to the students that even though we are citizens of an earthly country, we must remember that God is Lord of all. We belong to an eternal king whose love and reign will never end. We demonstrate that Jesus is the king of our lives when we surrender our own rival kingdoms and acknowledge that we don't want to be the lord of our life; we want God to be the Lord of our life.

Make a paper crown to illustrate this theme. Choose a piece of heavy paper to use as the base of the crown and cut a strip 2" wide by 22" long. Make sure the strip is long enough to go around the head, with a little extra for overlapping and pasting. Glue the ends of the strip together to form a headband.

Cut twenty strips of construction paper—the same or different colors—making each one about one inch wide and ten inches long. Write one way to demonstrate citizenship in God's kingdom on each piece. Ideas to include may be: follow the Ten Commandments; respect God's creation; study God's Word; listen to parents; share with others; make peace during conflicts; pray on a regular basis.

Loop the strips in half without making creases and staple the two ends together inside the headband. Staple one strip right next to the other, until the headband is filled with loops.

Decorate the headband with trims. Apply various shaped stickers, cut and glue construction paper illustrations, or draw designs with markers. Wear the completed crowns and share in a closing prayer based on the words of The Apostles' Creed (see next page).

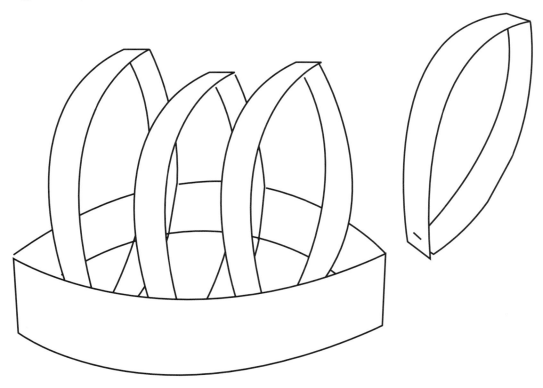

Ascension Day Prayer

Reader   Jesus rose from the dead.

ALL   Alleluia!

Reader   Jesus ascended into heaven.

ALL   Alleluia!

Reader   Jesus is seated at the right hand of God the Father.

ALL   Alleluia!

Reader   Jesus will come again in glory to judge the living and the dead.

ALL   Alleluia!

Reader   The kingdom of Jesus will have no end.

ALL   Alleluia!

Celebrating Cultural Diversity

Goal

To highlight the spirit of all God's people by holding an ethnic festival and prayer service to celebrate cultural diversity.

Gather

- Posterboard
- Markers
- Scissors
- Ethnic foods
- Cassette or CD player(s)
- Tables
- Book of world flags
- List of the word "peace" written in various languages
- Construction paper
- Glue sticks
- Rulers
- Ethnic stories
- Ethnic music
- Tablecloths
- Bible(s)

Advance Preparation

- Organize components of an ethnic festival such as displays, flags, foods, music, and stories.

Optional Activity

- Purchase and plant a Peace Pole. Order from:
    The Peace Pole Makers USA
    3534 West Lanham Road
    Maple City, MI 49664
    (231) 334-4567
    www.peacepoles.com
- Prepare the ground where the Peace Pole will be placed. Have on hand a shovel, basin, and water for planting the pole.

Guide

Pentecost, a Jewish festival of thanksgiving for harvested crops, was one of three major feasts celebrated by the people of Jesus' time. During Pentecost, commemorated fifty days after the feast of Passover, people from many nations gathered in Jerusalem for this annual event. Fifty days after Jesus' resurrection on Easter Sunday, during the observance of the festival of Pentecost, the Holy Spirit descended on the crowd and filled them with God's power and presence.

As a way of celebrating Pentecost, the feast of the Spirit's descent on all God's people, hold an ethnic festival on or near Pentecost Sunday. To begin the process, discuss how people are alike and how they are different. Differences in ethnic groups include language, skin color, food, clothes, music, and religious beliefs. Next, discuss ways that people are alike. All people have a basic human need for food, clothing and shelter. All people are part of the human race, the family of God.

No matter what a person's ethnic background, everyone requires compassion, love, and respect. All individuals need family and friends. All people feel joy and pain and all people laugh and cry. Diversity needs to be celebrated, and Pentecost offers an opportunity to highlight this theme.

Invite the class to decide on several different countries to highlight during the event. Some of the cultures should represent the ethnic backgrounds of the people in the group, in the congregation, and in the community. Choose countries that will reflect the diversity of all God's people rather than just a few nationalities. Also discuss possible components of a festival such as decorations, displays, entertainment, and food.

Begin by making flags to represent the countries that will be featured at the festival. Locate pictures of the flags in reference books. Use a full sheet of posterboard for the background of each flag and provide construction paper, markers, glue sticks, scissors, and rulers to add details and decorations.

Discuss foods to serve at the festival, for example, tacos for Mexico, rice for Asia, soda bread for Ireland, scones for England, rice and beans for Central America, banana bread for Africa, and potato pancakes for Germany. Decide who will be responsible for bringing the food. Also arrange for people to share music and stories from the various countries throughout the festivities. Obtain items representing the various cultures to display on the tables.

Just before the event, set up the tables in the area where the festival will take place and cover them with colorful cloths. Identify each table by hanging the country's flag on the wall or suspending it from the ceiling. Display books and information about the country on the table. Set up the food samples, together with plates, napkins, forks, knives, spoons, and serving pieces and utensils. Invite one or two participants to be responsible for welcoming guests to each table.

Play ethnic music and share stories throughout the event. Encourage people to wander through the festival to look at the flags, to view the displays, to taste the foods, to listen to the music, and to hear stories about different cultures. Allow time for everyone to enjoy all aspects of the event.

Conclude the celebration by gathering the participants for a prayer service.

Opening Song

Peace Is Flowing Like a River

Opening Prayer

Reader	Come give us your peace, a peace that the world does not know.
ALL	"Peace I give to you, my own peace I give you," says the Lord.
Reader	Lead all your creation to the river of peace, refresh us, restore us, give us your spirit.
ALL	"Peace I give to you, my own peace I give you," says the Lord.
Reader	We stand before you as one body in Christ, give to us a spirit of justice.
ALL	"Peace I give to you, my own peace I give you," says the Lord.
Reader	Let mercy and compassion flow from us like a never-ending stream.
ALL	"Peace I give to you, my own peace I give you," says the Lord.
Reader	We lift up our hands to the God of all creation; we bless you for all time.
ALL	"Peace I give to you, my own peace I give you," says the Lord.

Invite participants to say the word "peace" in their native languages or to read it in a different language.

Bless us as we commit ourselves to the effort of restoring order to one another and to the world. Amen. (*Continue on to next page for response.*)

Scripture Response   *Daniel 3:57–87*

Divide the group into two sides.

Right Side   Bless the Lord, all you works of the Lord.
Praise and exalt him above all forever.
All you waters above the heavens, bless the Lord.
All you hosts of the Lord, bless the Lord.
Sun and moon, bless the Lord.
Stars of heaven, bless the Lord.

Left Side   Every shower and dew, bless the Lord.
All you winds, bless the Lord.
Fire and heat, bless the Lord.
Cold and chill, bless the Lord.
Frost and rain, bless the Lord.
Ice and snow, bless the Lord.
Nights and days, bless the Lord.
Lightning and clouds, bless the Lord.

Right Side   Let the earth bless the Lord
Praise and exalt him above all forever.
Mountains and hills, bless the Lord.
Everything growing from the earth, bless the Lord.
You springs, bless the Lord.
All water creatures, bless the Lord.
All you birds of the air, bless the Lord.
All you beasts, wild and tame, bless the Lord.

Left Side   O Israel, bless the Lord.
Praise and exalt him above all forever.
Servants of the Lord, bless the Lord.
Spirits and souls of the just, bless the Lord.
Holy people of humble heart, bless the Lord.
Praise and exalt him above all forever.

All   Let us bless the Father, and the Son, and the Holy Spirit.
Let us praise and exalt them above all forever.
Blessed are you, Lord, in the firmament of heaven.
Praiseworthy and glorious and exalted above all forever.

If you are planting a Peace Pole, add this to your prayer service.

Planting the Peace Pole

Reader   Make this ground holy as a gift of your creation to us your people.

ALL   "Peace I give to you, my own peace I give you," says the Lord.

Invite the participants to extend their hands over the ground.

Reader   God of our redemption, Spirit of our lives, we call upon you now to make holy this ground on which we stand. Allow it to bring life and growth to body and soul in a spirit of peace and tranquility for all of your created order. We plant this Peace Pole today as a reminder of our own commitment to work for peace in our personal lives and in the world.

Lower the Peace Pole into the ground. As this takes place one person should move through the crowd with a basin of water. Invite the participants to take water in their hands and to sprinkle it onto the pole as a sign of blessing. Continue this process until everyone has had an opportunity to bless the Peace Pole.

Reader   The peace of the Lord be with you.

All   And also with you.

Invite the participants to share a sign of peace with one another.

Closing Song

Peace Is Flowing Like a River

Honoring the Spirit

Goal

To celebrate Pentecost in the spirit of a Native American prayer service.

Gather

- Bible(s)
- Wind chimes
- Candle
- Table
- Soil in a bowl
- Pitcher filled with water
- Cassette or CD player
- Cassette or CD of Native American music
- Water
- Basket
- Matches
- Tablecloth

Advance Preparation

- Set up a table in the center of the gathering space and cover it with a tablecloth.
- Invite four readers to offer prayers to the East, North, South, and West during the service.

Guide

"When the day of Pentecost had come, they were all together in one place. And suddenly from heaven there came a sound like the rush of a violent wind, and it filled the entire house where they were sitting. Divided tongues, as of fire, appeared among them, and a tongue rested on each of them. All of them were filled with the Holy Spirit and began to speak in other languages, as the Spirit gave them ability." (Acts 2:1–4) "So those who welcomed his message were baptized." (Acts 2:41a)

On Pentecost, the Spirit of God enlivened all of creation. People from all regions of the world—East, North, South, and West—were empowered with the presence of God. All of creation was once again made sacred through the power of the Spirit.

During the season of Pentecost emphasize the symbols of the story—air (wind), earth (place), fire (tongues), and water (baptism)—and their connection to Native American spirituality. Use a prayer service that has its focus in the Native American tradition of the Four Winds—East, North, South, and West—to celebrate the earth and all her blessings. Each of these directions is related to an element of creation: East, air; North, earth; South, fire; West, water.

Call to Prayer

As the service begins, play tranquil Native American music. Invite the participants to stand in a circle around the prayer table.

Reader	Loving God of all creation, come to our assistance.
ALL	Help us to renew the earth.
Reader	Let compassion kindle our hearts, and let integrity blaze like a flame of love.
ALL	Help us to renew the earth.
Reader	Rise, eternal winds, raise your hand, and do not forget your creation. You, yourself have seen and heard the groaning of creation. Heed what you hear.
ALL	Help us to renew the earth.
Reader	Eternal wind, you listen to the wants of your creation. Send water to the earth and fill the air with the fire of your Spirit. We pray because we believe.
ALL	Help us to renew the earth.

All turn toward the South.

Reader 1   We call and invite your presence, Spirit of the South.

Set the candle on the prayer table and use a match to light it.

Reader 1   You bring the warming winds of summer to touch our face, to soothe and heal our bodies. The south is characterized by heat, fire, and energy. Its colors are red, orange, and yellow. Great Spirit of the South, we send blessings and prayers to your people below the equator. Set the oppressed free and bring justice to all your people.

All turn toward the West.

Reader 2   We call and invite your presence, Spirit of the West.

Place the pitcher of water on the prayer table.

Reader 2   You bring the cooling of the setting sun and the comfort of the night. You enfold us with the great mystery of night and the lessons it brings to us. You refresh us with cool water when we are thirsty. The West is characterized by twilight and autumn. Its colors are shades of blue, purple, and green, the colors of the night sky and the waters that touch it. Great Spirit of the West, we send blessings and prayers to your Western people, the people of the water and the twilight.

All turn toward the North.

Reader 3   We call and invite your presence, Spirit of the North.

Set the basket of soil on the prayer table.

Reader 3   You are the cold wind that brings us back to reality. It is your Spirit of the North that brings the snows of winter with icy fury. With it you bring solitude to your creation. In the solitude of winter the seeds lie beneath the earth with the hope of new life. The North is characterized by mystery because it is never reached by the sun; it speaks to what is unknown. Because of its power and mystery the North represents the earth, midnight, winter, and darkness. Great Spirit of the North, we send blessings and prayers to your people of winter.

All turn toward the East.

Reader 4   We call and invite your presence, Spirit of the East.

Bring forward the wind chimes.

Reader 4   You are the color of the sky and you usher in a new day on the breeze. Spirit of the East, with the sunrise you bring new beginnings, like that of the springtime, new breath and life. You are characterized by the pale colors of the dawn. Spirit of the East, we send blessings and prayers to your people of the morning sky.

Reader   To conclude our prayer experience, each person is invited to come forward, one by one, to hold their hands over the candle flame, to touch the water, to feel the soil, and to shake the wind chimes as a form of blessing.

Allow time for each person to take a turn.

Reader   The peace of the Lord be with you.

ALL   And also with you.

Invite those gathered to share a sign of peace.

Learning About Missions

Goal

To emphasize the global nature of Pentecost through a traveling suitcase project.

Gather

- Suitcase
- Pens
- Prayer guide
- Mission project information
- Diary, journal, or notebook

- Class list
- Letter to parents
- Bible(s)
- Items from selected countries

Guide

Since the story of Pentecost emphasizes the global nature of the gospel, involve the children in an interesting, inexpensive trip around the world.

To highlight specific places in which the good news of God's love is being shared, or world missions in general, use items from these locations and offer students the opportunity to explore them in a unique format. Pack the articles in a suitcase which can then travel from child to child from week to week.

Before beginning the project, decide if one country at a time will be featured in the materials, or if a variety of items from places around the world will be showcased in the bag. If the learning experi-ence is designed to help the class members discover more about a place where a church supported missionary ministers, focus on one country at a time.

Gather items to place in the suitcase such as a map, flag, language book or tape, and historical information on the location. Clothing, hats, shoes, toys, and food products could also be packed. Information on a specific mission project and the people who serve in this place should be included. Materials and letters sent by the missionaries would be welcome additions to the case.

Provide a variety of books for the children to review. Resources on the country, a Bible in the nation's language, and magazines from or about the land would be interesting contents for the suitcase. Be sure to select books that reflect a wide range of reading skills and those with illustrations from which the young people can gather accurate information. Include a notebook, diary, or journal in the traveling bag and invite the children to write their comments as they explore the items.

Attach a letter to parents inside the lid of the suitcase requesting that they read the stories with their child and that they talk together about the pictures and other items in the case.

Remind the children of the importance of praying every day for missions, both near and far. Develop a prayer guide to use in the suitcase. Here are some examples:

Sunday: *world*
- Pray for people around the world.
- Pray for those who deliver food, clothing, and medical supplies to missions throughout the world.

Monday: *country*
- Pray for the people of your own country.
- Pray for doctors and nurses who do volunteer work with missions in this country.

Tuesday: *state*
- Pray for the people in your state.
- Pray for teachers and other volunteers who work in a literacy program.

Wednesday: *community*
- Pray for the people in your city or town.
- Pray for the people who direct homeless shelters, food banks, and halfway houses.

Thursday: *parish*
- Pray for the people in your parish.
- Pray for those in the parish who lead and assist in outreach and social support ministries.

Friday: *family*
- Pray for the people in your family.
- Pray for the parents, guardians, and other adults who try to set a good example for children.

Saturday: *self*
- Pray for yourself.
- Pray for young people who act as missionaries in their school, parish, and local community.

Encourage the students to use the missions prayer guide to develop their own petitions for use now and in the future.

Make a list of the children's names and let each person in the class take the suitcase home for a week. Put a check by the child's name when the suitcase is taken, and another check when the bag is returned. When everyone has had the opportunity to explore the items from one country, begin the project again with materials from a new place.

Sensing the Season

Goal

To use the five senses to create a dramatization of the first Pentecost experience.

Gather

- Bible(s)
- Incense holder
- Basket
- Bread
- Six dancers
- Woven or textured tablecloth
- Candles (twelve in a variety of colors and sizes)
- Cassette tape or CD of wind sounds
- Cassette or CD player
- "Pentecost" phrases in different languages
- Incense
- Matches
- Grapes
- Table
- White robes (for dancers)

Advance Preparation

- Create the environment for the prayer service in a large area with ample room for movement throughout the space.
- Set the unlit candles around the room.
- Position the tablecloth on the floor in the center of the space. Arrange the bread and the grapes in a basket and set the container in the center of the tablecloth.
- Put the incense stick in a holder and place it on the cloth.
- Prepare to play the wind sounds and place the equipment out of sight.
- Select a helper to play the recording on cue.
- Select a phrase for the dancers to chant, for example:

    I am sending you My Spirit;

    I am your God and I am with you;

    Love one another as I have loved you;

    The Spirit will fill your hearts with abounding love.

  Translate the sentence into different languages, if possible.

Guide

Use the senses to experience the season of Pentecost through sight, smell, sound, taste, and touch. Welcome the children as they arrive and invite them to sit on the floor around the prayer table. Explain that the group will recreate the story of Pentecost in a unique way: by using their senses. Read the account of Pentecost, Acts 2:1–4 (or verses 1–42), now or at a later time.

Ask the students their names and where they live. If all participants are from the same city, ask them to state their addresses. Highlight the fact that everyone is from a different place, much like the crowd assembled in Jerusalem for the feast of Pentecost.

Once the introductions are completed, light the candles and the incense. Then encourage the group to share stories about their friend Jesus. Guide the discussion with questions such as: what do you remember about Jesus? What did Jesus do while he was on earth? What did Jesus say? Who did Jesus help? While the stories are shared, pass the basket of bread and grapes and enjoy the food together.

At a predetermined time, approximately ten to fifteen minutes into the storytelling, a helper should turn on the recording of wind sounds. Give the participants time to realize that they are listening to the sound of wind.

After a moment or two the white-robed people should dance into the room speaking in different languages. To simulate chaos, the chanting and movement should take place at the same time. Each dancer should repeat the same phrase in a different language. At some point the dancers should encourage the participants to get up and to join the movement.

Once the participants are reseated, the robed dancers should gracefully move out of the room. Invite the learners to discuss what just took place. Explain that the group experienced the story of Pentecost through sight, smell, sound, taste, and touch.

(The twelve candles which provided light in the room also symbolized the twelve disciples; the bread and grapes offered a taste of the Last Supper or an agape meal that the followers of Jesus might have shared; the incense heightened the sense of smell; the chanted phrases, storytelling, and wind sounds stimulated the sense of hearing; the dancers accentuated the sense of touch.)

Allow time to process the experience or to read or re-read the Pentecost account from the Bible. Then invite the participants to join hands for a closing prayer.

Closing Prayer

Creator, Redeemer, and Spirit God, you fill our very souls with the wind of your love. Help us to share your love and peace through a compassionate understanding of each other.

Thank you for sending Jesus as our redeemer and the Spirit as our helper and guide. Open our hearts to the power of these awesome gifts. Awaken our senses to experience you through sight, smell, sound, taste, and touch. Amen.

Suggested Resources

Bragdon, Allen D., Editor, produced in cooperation with the United States Committee for UNICEF. *Joy through the World*. New York: Dodd, Mead, 1985.

Costello, Gwen. *Classroom Prayer Services for the Days of Advent and Lent*. Mystic, CT: Twenty-Third Publications, 1999.

Ehret, Walter and George K. Evans. *The International Book Of Christmas Carols*. Brattleboro, VT: Stephen Greene Press, 1980.

Fowler, Virginia. *Christmas Crafts and Customs Around the World*. New York: Prentice-Hall, 1984.

Kielly, Shiela and Sheila Geraghty. *Advent & Lent Activities for Children: Camels, Carols, Crosses, and Crowns*. Mystic, CT: Twenty-Third Publications, 1999.

Liechty, Anna L., Phyllis Vos Wezeman, and Judith Harris Chase. *The Christmas Story A-Z*. Prescott, AZ: Educational Ministries, Inc., 1992.

Maxwell, Bernard J., Judy Foster & Jill Shirvington. *Easter for 50 Days*. Mystic, CT: Twenty-Third Publications, 1989.

Neuberger, Anne. *Advent Stories and Activities: Meeting Jesus through the Jesse Tree*. Mystic, CT: Twenty-Third Publications, 1999.

O'Neal, Debbie Trafton and David LaRochelle, illustrator. *Before and After Easter*. Minneapolis, MN: Augsburg, 1992.

Rust, Henry, editor. *Celebrating Holy Week*. Prescott, AZ: Educational Ministries, Inc., 1993.

Schneider, Valerie. *Teaching Sacraments and Seasons: Reflections, Prayers & Activities for Religion Teachers*. Mystic, CT: Twenty-Third Publications, 1999.

Smith, Judy Gattis. *Birth, Death, and Resurrection: Teaching Spiritual Growth Through the Church Year*. Nashville: Abingdon, 1989.

Wezeman, Phyllis Vos. *52 Bible Stories in Rhyme and Rhythm*. Carthage, IL: Shining Star, 1995.

——*Holy Week: Experiencing the Events through Art Activities*. Prescott, AZ: Educational Ministries, Inc., 1992.

Wezeman, Phyllis Vos and Jude Dennis Fournier. *Advent Alphabet*. Prescott, AZ: Educational Ministries, Inc., 1989.

——*Counting The Days: Twenty Five Ways*. Prescott, AZ: Educational Ministries, Inc., 1989.

——*Joy to the World*. Notre Dame, IN: Ave Maria Press, 1992.

——*Lenten Alphabet*. Prescott, AZ: Educational Ministries, Inc., 1993.

Wezeman, Phyllis Vos and Anna L. Liechty. *Hymn Stories For Children: Special Days and Holidays*. Grand Rapids, MI: Kregel Publications, 1994.

——*Hymn Stories for Children: The Christmas Season*. Grand Rapids, MI: Kregel Publications, 1997.

Wezeman, Phyllis Vos, Anna L. Liechty, and Judith Harris Chase. *Church Season: Volume One, Volume Two, Volume Three, Volume Four*. Mishawaka, IN: Active Learning Associates, Inc., 1996, 1997, 1998, 1999.

——*Sense the Season! A Resource For Advent, Christmas & Epiphany*. Prescott, AZ: Educational Ministries, Inc., 1999.

Wilson, Jan and Linda Herd, illustrator. *Feasting for Festivals*. Batavia, IL: Lion, 1990.

Zyromski, Page McKean. *Echo Stories for Children: Celebrating Saints and Seasons in Word and Action*. Mystic, CT: Twenty-Third Publications, 1998.

Of Related Interest...

Advent Stories and Activities

Meeting Jesus through the Jesse Tree
Anne E. Neuberger

Twenty-four ancient stories and symbols (from creation to the nativity) mark the days before Christmas. Introduce children (7-12) to the tradition of keeping a Jesse Tree with easy-to-follow directions for creating seven types of trees to accommodate various settings, time constraints, and abilities.

96 pages, $12.95 (order B-22)

Advent & Lent Activities for Children

Camels, Carols, Crosses, and Crowns
Shiela Kielly and Sheila Geraghty

Here's everything teachers, catechists, and parents ever wanted to know about Advent and Lent customs and traditions, as well as suggestions for sharing this information with children (ages 6–11).

128 pages $9.95 (order M-51)

Classroom Prayer Services for the Days of Advent and Lent

Gwen Costello

Sixty creative services involve children (7-12) in celebrating God's presence through processions, veneration of the Bible, prayer patterns, speaking parts, guided meditations, and blessings. Catholic customs are also presented. Easily incorporated into lesson plans.

144 pages, $12.95 (order B-39)

Celebrating Catholic Rites and Rituals in Religion Class

Kathy Chateau and Paula Miller

These celebrations unfold our basic ritual signs as Christians: the gathering of the assembly, signing with the cross, naming, blessing, laying on of hands, anointing with oil, and more. Each chapter includes: background information about the ritual; a variety of ways it can be used; the necessary preparations and suggestions regarding materials; and, of course, the ritual itself. An indispensable resource for DREs, catechists, teachers, children's catechumenate directors, and families of children in the catechumenate.

80 pages, $9.95 (order J-01)

Echo Stories for Children

Celebrating Saints and Seasons in Word and Action
Page McKean Zyromski

Twenty delightful stories involve students (ages 5–11) by inviting them to mirror the teacher's words and actions. Focuses on biblical characters and religious and seasonal feasts; includes class discussion questions and a closing prayer.

168 pages, $19.95 (order B-76)

Available at religious bookstores or from:

TWENTY-THIRD PUBLICATIONS

PO BOX 180 · 185 WILLOW STREET   MYSTIC, CT 06355 · 1-800-321-0411
FAX: 1-800-572-0788   BAYARD   E-MAIL: ttpubs@aol.com

Call for a free catalog